PLANET EARTH

AS HUMAN BEINGS,
WHERE DID WE COME FROM?
WHY ARE WE HERE?

Rev. Jay Samonie, Ph.D.

Books by the same author:

1.   On My Way Home

2.   Reflections on My Way Home

3.   My Greatest Joys on My Way Home

4.   The Holy Spirit: Our Divine
      Companion Guiding Us on Our Way
      Home.

5.   The Rite of Passage

PLANET EARTH

AS HUMAN BEINGS,
WHERE DID WE COME FROM?
WHY ARE WE HERE?

Rev. Jay Samonie, Ph.D.

Library of Congress Control Number: 2008902223

ISBN: 978-0-9752636-3-1

Art work on cover design, from a painting by Rev. Jay Samonie, PhD.

Printed in the United States by:
Morris Publishing
3212 East Highway 30
Kearney, NE 68847
800-650-7888

PREFACE

Planet Earth is a planet of dreams and the illusion of being separated from our Creator and from each other. That is why we have World Wars and so much crime, violence and conflict between cities and villages in the world.

Helping to alleviate this condition of separation, on December 4, 2007, Jimmy and Rosalynn Carter started the Carter Center. Its purpose was to fight disease and build hope around the world. The Center has worked closely with more than 70 countries. In 1986, the Guinea worm disease affected 3.5 million people who drank impure water that left them temporarily crippled. Another 120 million were at risk. River Blindness infected over 18 million men, women and children with 123 million at risk. The Carter Center is still countering these diseases.

More than 3,600,000 African families in Ethiopia and Malawi were taught skills and knowledge to double and triple their crops. The Carter Center also focused on fair elections. It personally monitored the voting process in Palestine, Indonesia, Ethiopia, Venezuela and China.

Whether fighting disease, reducing hunger or advancing peace and democracy, the Authorities of every country, at some point, will have to help solve the complex and difficult problems faced by the poorest and most defenseless among us.

Although there are several races and many different religions and cultures in the world, **all of us, without exception, are Siblings as God's Divine Children**... and it is impossible to be separated from God or from each other. Anything else is an **illusion.**

AUTHOR'S NOTES

1. I was ordained a priest in 1956.

2. I spent 25 years of my priestly ministry in the inner city of Detroit, Michigan.

3. As Pastor of Most Holy Trinity, each year my Counselors and I assisted over 30,000 people who were poor and came to us for help.

4. The poor families were of many origin: Hispanic, African, Indian, Cuban, Puerto Rican and Caucasian.

5. I was the only Catholic Priest ever to serve on the Judicial Tenure Commission, evaluating the conduct of Judges on the bench for the Supreme Court in the State of Michigan.

6. I have had a wide range of religious and practical experience, having served as Pastor in several

parishes from 1963 until 1995. I continued helping as a retired priest in five different churches until 2004, when I had two severe heart attacks, Congestive Heart Failure several times and a stroke.

ACKNOWLEDGMENTS

Richard and Kathy Rice, who helped me to set up the book margins in the correct and Camera-ready format for publication and fixed my manuscript when something malfunctioned. It would have been very difficult to complete my manuscript without their assistance.

Jack and Ronnie Morgan, who proofread the entire manuscript.

Sally Owen, who encouraged me to pursue this topic about living on Planet Earth. She also assisted in organizing the material.

THIS BOOK IS DEDICATED TO

My Sister, Lillian Simony, who left this world and was called to heaven in 2007, four days before her 90th Birthday Party. She was a very gentle and loving person who never spoke unkindly about anyone. She had great devotion to the Mother of Jesus and said her Rosary daily.

My sister Lillian had a perfect death. She was talking with my sister Billie on the telephone with her son Jerry at her side. She stopped talking, gently laid her head back and was called to Heaven.

TABLE OF CONTENTS

PREFACE 7

AUTHOR'S NOTES 9

ACKNOWLEDGMENTS 11

DEDICATION 12

1. IS LIFE ON PLANET EARTH ALL THERE IS? 15

2. THE STAGE IS BEING SET FOR THE ORIGIN OF THE HUMAN RACE . . . 24

3. ARE THERE HUMAN BEINGS EVERYWHERE IN THE UNIVERSE? . 35

4. WHAT DO WE KNOW ABOUT THE SON OF GOD? 50

5. TODAY, SOME BIBLE SCHOLARS CHALLENGE THE RESURRECTION OF JESUS FROM THE DEAD 59

6. GOD'S ETERNAL, UNIVERSAL AND UNCHANGEABLE LAWS 72

7. WHAT IS THE EGO AND ITS UNREAL WORLD? 83

8. THIS IS HOW "A COURSE IN MIRACLES" BEGINS 92

TABLE OF CONTENTS

9. WHO WAS WILLIAM SHAKESPEARE? . 107

10. EINSTEIN: SCIENCE, MATH AND
    RELIGION 117

11. PLANET EARTH IS LIKE A BUSY
    AIRPORT WITH SOULS DREAMING OF
    EXPERIENCE 126

12. EACH OF US HAS TO DECIDE
    BETWEEN TWO OPPOSITE THOUGHT
    SYSTEMS AS A WAY OF LIFE . . . 137

13. PROJECTION MAKES PERCEPTION . 144

14. DOES *TIME* EXIST AS BILLIONS OF
    YEARS? 155

15. FORGIVENESS: THE KEY TO
    FREEDOM 164

16. AN ACTUAL AND SURPRISING EYE
    WITNESS TO THE ONENESS OF
    GOD'S SON 174

17. SINCE PLANET EARTH IS NOT
    REAL, WE NEED DIVINE HELP TO
    GUIDE US HOME 179

18. EVOLUTION OR INTELLIGENT
    DESIGN? 197

CHAPTER 1

IS LIFE ON PLANET EARTH ALL THERE IS?

As a child, I grew up like any other kid on the block. I would think big in terms of family since I was number ten out of eleven children, but I grew up in a small neighborhood on the lower east side of Detroit, Michigan. There was never a question of why we were here. I took the world for granted. I believed that we were all dealt certain cards and that was our life! Some were lucky; they had the good life. Others were destined to a life without hope, being plagued by an incurable illness or poverty. I knew friends personally who were handicapped and the majority of people living there were poor.

Fortunately, something happened to me that people on this planet never talked about. When I was just seven years old, I knew there was another world...a spirit world beyond this one. I had a vision with my brother Tony (of happy memory) and two of my sisters: Rose and Elizabeth. The four of us had a vision of this incredible world over and above Mt. Elliott Cemetery, which was just across the street from our parents' grocery store. We stared through the window with unbelievable amazement and awe for almost an hour. The spirit world we witnessed was teeming with life and activity. It was far above and beyond anything we could have ever imagined on this physical planet we call Earth.

In spite of this discovery, I still thought of Planet Earth as the real thing. It was home! It was solid, stable and something we could see, feel and touch. The Earth was a place in which we experienced life with its good times and its sad times.

There was always a natural desire to continue living so that we could become seniors in society and enjoy the benefits of retirement. Our lives, of course, did not turn out that way! The truth was that we generally became vulnerable to the usual experiences of the elderly: needing medications which were very costly while living on a fixed income...and many of us did not have Health Insurance. We became subject to acquiring a certain fatal disease such as cancer, a life threatening virus, pneumonia, a heart attack, a stroke or some other sickness, ending in death. That's all there was!

My life, however, got turned around. When I was 14 years old, about to enter High School, a Voice spoke to me as I was walking to the open field where my buddies and I played baseball almost every day. The Voice encouraged me to follow a totally different path of life. This Voice was not in my mind... I could hear it with my ears. His words were not what I wanted to hear, but the Voice was very convincing. The Voice told me to take the test for entering Sacred Heart Seminary in Detroit Michigan in order to become a Catholic Priest. I realize now that it was the Voice of Jesus or the Holy Spirit.

I was just starting to like girls at that time; I had no thought of becoming a Catholic Priest. I jokingly said to myself, "Why didn't He call me to be a Protestant Clergyman?" That way, I could have been a Pastor or Minister of a Church, be married and have children.

I was just a kid! I had no thought of becoming a priest. All I wanted was to grow up and get married like my parents and have a lot of children. But the Voice, a very pleasant voice encouraged me at such a young age to dedicate my life to Christ in the Seminary...and remain unmarried in this lifetime. This was not my original desire. Yes, I enjoyed my classmates and other seminarians, but I was unhappy because I missed my family (Lebanese families are very close to one another). I also missed my mother's Lebanese cooking and her delicious baked goods.

It almost sounds humorous at this point in my life, but for **ten years in a row**, I had no intention of returning to the Seminary after our summer break, but the Voice always encouraged me to go back to Sacred Heart Seminary in the Fall. So I did, and was ordained as a Catholic Priest in 1956. I have been a Priest for more than fifty years. End of story!

I can say today that it is not the end of the story! Being seventy-seven years old and living in the year 2008, I have a totally different view of God and **Planet Earth.** I am going to start out with a couple of statements that may contradict everything you have ever believed about life in this world.

The first is: *God did not create our world called Planet Earth!* The second is: *Planet Earth is not real!*

You may be thinking that is not possible! "Fr. Jay has gone over the edge this time! We experience life here every day...every moment. The sun rises every morning whether we see it or not and there is without question a sunset every evening. We do not have to see it. The sun rises and sets every day without fail. Scientists say that the sun may have about five billion more years to shine and the Earth will be here millions of years after we experience death. These are scientific facts. They can be proven. We all know these basic and reliable truths."

So, how could I, Fr. Jay, make such wild statements about our home in this world and our life-giving sun? How can I deny the facts? I repeat and I will explain, shortly, that life here is not real. It is actually an ***illusion,*** *a* ***dream,*** *and for millions of people everywhere, a* ***nightmare.***

In general, even the Yoga Masters of India and the Master Teachers in the Far East referred to this world as **"maya"** or an illusion. They had many followers as they walked through different towns teaching intensely about the experience of life and death. Buddha, Confucius, Lao-tse, Krishna and other ancient Masters left us with remarkable words of wisdom. Still, they may not have been aware of the absolute origin of the human race.

I still stand behind my *wild* statements about life on this planet. Yes, our eyes see beautiful sunsets, gigantic mountain ranges, vast oceans, a stunning variety of beautiful flowers and a huge species of towering and colorful trees. *Yet, we cannot help noticing that everything we see with our eyes is changing or dying.*

NOTHING HERE IS *ETERNAL!* Everything will disappear some day. It is only a matter of time. Even the tall and invincible *ash trees* are dying by the thousands due to a tiny, insignificant beetle called the *ash borer* and more recently, *global warming* adds more fear to our uncertain future.

In January of 2008, the Detroit Free Press included an article about the Dengue Fever, a deadly virus which has already struck Hawaii, Texas and Puerto Rico. The World Health Organization estimates that more than 50 million cases of Dengue infection occur each year. They attribute the flu-like illness to an increase of global warming.

Our True History goes back much further than the Bible, the Koran or any ancient Scriptures such as the Vedas in the Far East. The true origin of the human race took place long before *time* and this universe began.

CHAPTER 2

THE STAGE IS BEING SET
FOR THE ORIGIN OF
THE HUMAN RACE

I have come to believe, while I was studying Metaphysics, that the **TRUE HISTORY OF PLANET EARTH AND THE ORIGIN OF THE HUMAN RACE TOOK PLACE IN 1965.** In that year, Jesus, the Son of God, delivered an accurate explanation of where the human race came from and why we believe we are on this planet.

The writers of the Old Testament, such as Moses, Isaiah and the Prophets of the Bible were truly inspired, as were the Disciples of the New Testament. Being inspired is precisely the difference between the *Bible* and the recent Message of Jesus. His Message was not just *inspired*. It was *DICTATED, word for word,* to the scribe, Helen

- 24 -

Schucman. The Son of God left no room for mere inspiration, and spoke of His Message as *A Course in Miracles*.

For Jesus to reveal the Absolute Truth about the human race, the right conditions were being set up. It began with the decision of two people (chosen by Jesus in advance) to join in a common goal. Helen Schucman and William Thetford were Professors of Medical Psychology at Columbia University's College of Physicians and Surgeons in New York City. They were not considered especially spiritual or religious and their relationship was, at times, difficult and overly stressful.

In general, like most people, they had believed and invested their lives in the values of this world. Their *willingness*, however, to join together with *one common goal* became a *sacred moment* or a *holy instant* which is like an open window to the Lord.

Helen was Jewish and she could not believe that Jesus had chosen her, of all people, to do this work. In the course of time, she came to believe very strongly in Our Lord Jesus Christ. He even told her that she was part of the plan to reveal the Truth long before the Earth began, and this was the right time!

Helen, in her own words, says this about herself: "I was working in a prestigious and highly academic setting. And then something happened that triggered a chain of events I could never have predicted. The head of my department unexpectedly announced that he was tired of the angry and aggressive feelings their attitudes reflected and concluded that *there must be another way*. As if on cue, I agreed to help him find it."

Apparently, Jesus' Message called *"A Course in Miracles"* was the other way. (From this point on, I shall, at times, simply call it The *Course*.) Although they had good intentions in achieving their goal, Helen and Bill continued to experience disagreement and friction in the beginning. They did not realize it at the time, but they had, perhaps with Divine Assistance, given the Holy Spirit and the Lord Jesus, a sufficient setting to enable Jesus to express the Truth about the human race.

Helen, referring to herself, said, "Three startling months preceded the actual writing, during which time Bill suggested that I write down the highly *symbolic dreams* and descriptions of the *strange images* that were coming to me. Although I had grown more accustomed to the unexpected by that time, I was still very surprised when I wrote, This is "*A Course in Miracles*." That was my introduction to the Voice.

"It made no sound, but seemed to be giving me a kind of rapid, inner dictation which I took down in a shorthand notebook. The writing was never automatic. It could be interrupted at any time and later picked up again. It made me very uncomfortable, but it never seriously occurred to me to stop. It seemed to be a special assignment I had somehow, somewhere agreed to complete. It represented a truly collaborative venture between Bill and myself and much of its significance, I am sure, lies in that. I would take down the exact words the Voice communicated to my mind, read it to Bill the next day and he typed it from my dictation. I suspect he also had his special assignment, but without his support and encouragement, I would never have been able to fulfill mine.

The whole process took about seven years. Only a few minor changes have been made. Chapter titles and subheadings have been inserted in the Text and some of the more personal references that occurred at the beginning have been omitted. Otherwise, none of the material is substantially changed."

The names of the collaborators do not appear on the cover, because the Course can and should stand on its own. It is not intended to become the basis for another cult. Its only purpose is to provide a way in which people seeking the Truth, will be able to find their own Heavenly Teacher.

As its title implies, The Course is arranged as a teaching device. It consists of three books: a 622-page

TEXT, a 478-page **WORKBOOK** for Students, and an 88-page **MANUAL FOR TEACHERS**. The order in which the students of The Course choose to use the books and the ways in which they study them, depend on their particular needs and preferences.

Jesus' Message about the origin of **Planet Earth** is more easily understood today now that the general public is aware of the difference between the conscious mind and the subconscious mind as the result of the many years of research by Sigmund Freud, Carl Jung and other well-known psychologists. Besides their research into the existence of the subconscious mind, they also published articles about the *ego*, including *defense mechanisms*, such as *denial* and *projection*.

The Course makes no claim to finality, nor are the *Workbook* lessons intended to bring the student's learning to completion. In the end, the reader is left in the hands of a personal Teacher (The Holy Spirit or the Lord Jesus), Who will direct and guide all subsequent learning as He sees fit. Truth cannot be limited to any temporary form or shape.

On March 18, 2004, I met with a group of friends studying *"A Course In Miracles"*. While we were discussing the Course, I mentioned the book, ***"The Disappearance of the Universe"***, by Gary Renard. I was impressed by the two Apostles, St. Thomas and St. Thaddeus materializing in front of Gary and quoting some very important texts from *"A Course in Miracles"*, making it easier to understand. Other books that were an inspiration to me were Thomas Merton's ***"New Seeds of Contemplation"*** and Neale Walsch's ***"Conversations with God."***

They all talk about God, although no one can adequately describe the Attributes of God, the Infinite, Eternal and Almighty Creator of all that is Eternal. There is only one perfect definition of God: *"God is!"*

I remember Joyce Haglethorn who conducted a program on television called *"Exploring the Psyche"*. I was on her program several times. She almost always asked me in **the interview on live television** in the very last 30 seconds of an hour program: "Give me a definition of God!" I remember saying "Joyce, you are doing that to me again. Okay, let me define God in the most perfect way possible with no flaws whatsoever in it. **"God is!"**

That's the way God defined Himself to Moses: *"I AM WHO I AM"* which equals *"GOD IS!"*. If I add something, like God is Perfect. Really! How Perfect? How much better is an Infinite God than we are. If I say God is all knowing. How much does God know? Does He know what's in the dictionary? Does He understand the latest advances in math and science? The truth is that we have no idea how much God knows. **My personal belief is that God knows everything!** In my Theology Courses in the Seminary, we used the word **"Omniscient"** which meant that God has Universal and complete Knowledge of all that exists. Of course, there is no way to adequately describe an Eternal Being. *God is all there is!* There is nothing else in the world or universe.

Why is God all there is? Because Only God is Real, Infinite, Ageless and Eternal. Jesus said in 1965, (in "A Course in Miracles"), that Nothing Real can be threatened. God and His *One Son* are the only Eternal Reality that can never be threatened.

Heaven is the *Natural State* of all the Children of God. *we are all, at this very moment, in God's Eternal Kingdom.* Such is our Reality forever. No one has actually left The Kingdom, including criminals and the devil himself. There are no exceptions! God is the Infinite Creator and we can only **dream** or have an ***illusion*** that we have left His Eternal Kingdom.

CHAPTER 3

ARE THERE HUMAN BEINGS EVERYWHERE IN THE UNIVERSE?

THE ANSWER IS YES! Where do these souls come from and where are they going?

The **conflict** between the Siblings (God's Children) who were determined to leave God's Eternal Kingdom and other more faithful Siblings who tried to persuade them to stay, ended in a place to hide from God for fear of being punished. The result was an **unreal** physical universe.

The last book of the Bible, *The Book of Revelation*, was written by St. John, an Apostle of Our Lord Jesus Christ. In Chapter 12:7-12, it says:

"Then war broke out in heaven; Michael and his Angels battled against the dragon (a symbol used for the leader of the fallen angels). The dragon and his angels fought back, but did not prevail and there was no longer a place for them in Heaven. The huge *dragon*, the ancient serpent, *who is called the Devil or Satan*, who deceived the whole world, was thrown down to earth and its angels were thrown down with it."

Then I heard a loud voice in Heaven say: "Now have salvation and power come, and the Kingdom of our God and the Authority of His Anointed(Jesus). For the accuser of our Brothers is cast out, who accuses them day and night. They defeated him by the blood of the Lamb. Therefore rejoice, you heavens and you who dwell in them. But woe to you, earth and sea (Planet Earth and the physical universe), for the Devil has come down to you in great fury, for he knows he has but a short time."

Is it any wonder that in Jewish History, Adam and Eve were tempted by a dragon, the ancient serpent, in the Garden of Eden?

The making of an unreal universe was merely the *fallen angels'* dream and a good place to hide from God for fear of being punished. Since it was only a *dream*, it was not real and God would not enter the dream or illusion of His Children.

Their dream turned out to be a faulty and a very poor imitation of God's Eternal Kingdom. **Planet Earth** is a part of that unreal universe. **Planet Earth** may have seemed **real** to the fallen angels and to us living on it today, but from the viewpoint of the Holy Spirit, the Lord Jesus and the Heavenly Father, it is not **Real**. Even though we are living in this **dream** or **illusion**, we still have *genuine experiences* that can be brief moments of happiness or times of doubts and fears that can be terribly painful.

Everything here is so uncertain, with millions of criminals in every country, crime in every city and the average person living in fear. Feeling alone in this world and believing that we are separate from God and from each other, adds to sleepless nights and frightening thoughts of possibly being threatened by violence, physical harm, sickness and death.

With the discovery of the computer, the world today is like a global village with live news being broadcast nonstop on the Internet. On the positive side, the Internet is bringing knowledge and a deeper understanding of those who differ from us by color, culture and creed. Today, we know a lot more about countries like Iraq, China, Japan, South America, Indonesia, Africa, etc., with up-to-date information and location.

Every carrier on the Internet wants to be the first to announce the latest worldwide News of a shocking, scandalous or frightening story. It is highly competitive!

The computer, however, offers certain dangerous programs which are easily available to teens and even to younger children. These programs can be very harmful in the wrong hands. Many seductive crimes have been committed though this type of communication.

Wouldn't it be sheer madness or insanity to think that God would create such an imperfect and dangerous world? Rather, it was the foolish work of some of God's Children who were **dreaming** of leaving the Kingdom of Heaven.

Those same Children kept dreaming and believing in such a mad and crazy idea. The right response should have been: "The Holy Spirit was right! There is nothing out there but God."

But they kept on dreaming! Soon, what they dreamed turned sour. They thought God would surely punish them, although the Heavenly Father would never punish His own Children who were still dreaming. In their fear, they knew one place where God would not find them.

They quickly separated from each other and scattered as individuals to an unreal universe. It was only a dream or an illusion. The Holy Spirit continued to remind them: "You never left God's Kingdom! Wake up!" They still did not respond. They covered themselves in shame, believing there was only one way Home - the long Way - through something they invented called *time!* Since it was merely a dream, *time* did not exist in their unreal universe. Unfortunately, we were born on that unreal universe and **Planet Earth** is a part of their dream or illusion. The Message of Jesus, speaking to all the souls, including ourselves, believing that we are on **Planet Earth** and have left God's Kingdom offers this reminder: ***"YOU ARE ON A JOURNEY WITHOUT DISTANCE TO A PLACE YOU HAVE NEVER LEFT."*** (This means we have never really left God's Eternal Kingdom!)

The circumstances of my personal belief system has greatly changed. Since 1965, the Lord Jesus ***DICTATED* the message, word for word, describing the origin of the human race.** Through His Message, we are living today in what may be called the Age of Enlightenment or Salvation! We have learned that God's Love for us, even though we are dreaming, is continuous and everlasting and so is His Presence.

We have never left God's Kingdom! The Lord Jesus updated our belief system when He stated: **"The Kingdom of Heaven is *within* you."** *(Some Bible translations say:* The Kingdom of Heaven is *among* you!) Either one reminds us of our True Origin!

ENLIGHTENMENT is a process of peeling back the layers of our ego/mind - like unrolling a carpet - to reveal the True and Divine Self that we are. It is a grand opportunity for us to experience **God's Eternal Universe** in all its beauty and dimensions. The truth of who we are abides in the **Spiritual Center of our Being** while we experience what we call **life**. However, it is regrettable that most people on **Planet Earth** are totally unaware that there is a deep stillness hidden within us.

Enlightenment is the constant realization of True Spiritual Knowledge and Inner Peace at the very Center and Core of our innermost Being. Abide in this Center and we will enjoy a life full of meaning, celebration, clear thinking and happiness.

Spiritual Enlightenment is a continuous realization that we are **Eternal Beings** who will never die. (Death is merely a transition from this life to **life in the spirit world!**) **WE ARE IMMORTAL!** This Truth comes from Knowledge beyond the body and the mind.

The Holy Spirit is within each of us, and It is like a living, breathing and conscious Intelligence that Loves each of us unconditionally. We achieve Salvation when we surrender to this Eternal Truth.

The following steps may take you closer to having **an experience of** *enlightenment.* You will begin to feel more spiritually awake and alive the more you apply one or more of these steps. Go easy on yourself. You may have been trying to experience these for a long time:

1. The feeling of being separate and disconnected from God's Universe. This is how you create failure after failure in life. This habitual illusion that you are *not* connected to the Divine, stems from the mind's attachment to the *ego.*

Like a computer, the ego just spits out information and computes ideas that are unreal. The ego/mind is a limited construction of ideas and beliefs about whom we think we are. The more we can silence the chattering mind, the less we are trapped in the ego thought system. We could say that E. G. O. is like an acronym: **Excluding God's Omnipresence!**

Only through the constant release of the Ego can we live in the true spiritually enlightened Reality.

Embrace and Release all your Fears. F.E.A.R. is another acronym: **False Evidence Appearing Real.** Run towards the Truth and embrace it and all unreal thoughts will dissolve at the perfect time.

2. Disregard any stories that emphasize the belief in separation. Most of us had parents who were often concerned about paying taxes and the daily bills for food, clothes and other items that had to be bought. Like our parents, we grew up believing that we were limited. As children, we never had classes in school that taught us **meditation** or **positive thinking**.

The School Authorities, at that time, were not aware of the power of **mind** and

emotions. Moreover, there was **never** a connection with our **Infinite Source** as part of our class schedule. The Schools operated under the mistaken belief that success and truth were all about status, money and career. Happily, there have been some advances since those days.

3. The reality is that True Success is defined by how fulfilled we are as one of God's Beloved Children. That is something we cannot get from our job, our income, our marriage, nor our Academic Diplomas or Degrees.

We were not taught that the secret of God's Universe is discovered in the *NOW* moment. This is by far the greatest success we can ever achieve: being at *ONE* with the Infinite, All-powerful and All-knowing Universal God Force.

Truth does not come easy! Life on **Planet Earth** happens to be a *natural*

disorder! It is like an uncontrollable roller coaster, because we do not know what our future will be nor do we know how to respond to each experience that occurs outside our little fish bowl. A fish inside a small fish bowl has no idea that there is a big world out there, surrounding the fish bowl and full of activity and life, beyond its wildest dreams.

We do the same thing! Through our daily use of television, newspapers and the latest books, we hide from God's Infinite Spirit and become confused and trapped in our minds about what life is like beyond this one.

4.   Letting go of the need to be right. A very wise question is: **"Do you wish to be right or happy?"** Instead of always being right or playing **"the victim"** role, we can respond to life with inspired actions. We all have felt

victimized at certain times. This stems from a lack of inner peace, power and playfulness which can later create a severe sickness, lack of *ease* *(or disease)* in the body. Playing the victim role does get good strokes from others who feel sorry for our pain and they send us their love. In this way, we stay hooked and asleep, dreaming of separation from the Infinite Source within us.

Many "human beings" on Planet Earth are really "human programmings", having the same thoughts day after day after day and following the same routine day after day. This creates a deep rut in life and the only way out of it is by being responsible for our thoughts and choosing more empowering actions.

5. Choose to remain conscious and creative in the mystery of life. Society abhors people who step out of

line, but all the news media agree on one thing: that everything you need to end your suffering is *outside* of you, not *within* you! That's how the newspapers or a typical pharmacy will sell you unnecessary pills, ointments and cure-all remedies for colds, etc.

Choosing to be conscious, means waking up from fear and guilt. It takes a lot of effort to act against all our friends and family traditions to awaken. God's Divine and Eternal Love will not let us sleep forever or completely forget our True Nature. If we do not choose to wake up while we are still alive (in our physical body), God will let us know when our physical journey on Earth is over, and we will definitely know how much the Heavenly Father loves us, in more ways than we can possibly imagine.

CHAPTER 4

WHAT DO WE KNOW ABOUT THE SON OF GOD?

In **Chemistry,** He turned water into wine.

In **Biology,** He was born beyond normal conception.

In **Physics,** He defied the Law of Gravity when He ascended into heaven.

In **Economics,** He defied the Law of Return and Mathematics by feeding 5,000 followers with only two fishes and five loaves of bread.

In **Medicine,** He cured the sick and the blind without administering a single dose of drugs.

In **History,** He is in the *Center of Human History*, measuring *time* before and after His Birth. As God's Son, He is the beginning and the end.

In **Government,** He is called wonderful Counselor and Prince of peace.

In **Religion,** He said that no one comes to the Father except through Him.

Who is He? *He is the Lord Jesus:*

THE GREATEST PERSON EVER TO WALK ON THE FACE OF THE EARTH!

Jesus had no servants, yet they called Him Master.

He had no Academic Degrees, yet they called Him Teacher

He used no medicines, yet they called Him Healer.

He had no army, yet kings feared Him...

He won no military battles, yet He conquered the world.

He committed no crime, yet He allowed his enemies to condemn Him to death by Crucifixion.

He was buried in a tomb, yet He still lives today and promised to be with us until the end of the world.

Every person on Planet Earth has the Lord Jesus Christ and the Holy Spirit as Guides on our journey Home.

When Jesus said "The Father and I are one" and that "when you see Me you see the Father", He was speaking for all of us, His Siblings and the Children of God. But Jesus also said: "The Father is greater than I." True, the Father is greater than Jesus, God's favored Son, and all of us as Siblings.

In the *Message of Jesus, also called* "*A Course in Miracles*", it says: "God's Love sustains me and there is nothing to be afraid of." I have complete trust in the message of Jesus. There is nothing to fear under the Guidance of Jesus and the Holy Spirit.

If I were flying to Europe tomorrow, I would have no reason to experience *fear*. Does that mean that nothing bad can happen to me? I have no idea what would happen! If I have God's Eternal Love, it does not matter what happens. If death occurred, I would simply leave this play or stage that Shakespeare speaks of and go Home, which we call Heaven.

Sometimes, when I was younger and used to conduct funeral services, I felt a little envy toward the person who died. That person finished his or her work here and will be rewarded in heaven. That seemed, for a moment, rather attractive to me with my overly-busy schedule!

When one of my sisters died, I heard a couple of friends complain that it was too bad she was unable to go with the family to our annual reunion in Las Vegas. I said, "Too bad! We're talking about going to heaven. Las Vegas could never be compared to union with God! All Las Vegas wants is your money!" Being in a Casino is also a big distraction to each of us as the Loving Children of God.

They didn't realize what a wonderful thing it is to go Home. We are the ones stuck here in this **dream.** This **nightmare.** What we call life is temporary and vulnerable... and not even real. We are in a dreadful play on the stage of an imperfect world.

You know who knew this before all of us: The People in the Orient. The Master Teachers of India, China and the Monks of Tibet. They knew the difference. They even said that our dream life is more real than our life awake. They considered this life a nightmare operated by the ego system. Whenever the Bible uses the word devil or Satan or any power against God's power, you could substitute the word **ego**. The ego is the troublemaker and it is a thought system that some of our Siblings made up.

We are all Siblings who make up the Christ. That is all God created: His image and likeness, which is called **the Christ** (or God's Children) in the Eternal Kingdom, which includes all of us. **WE ARE THE CREATION OF GOD!**

The angels who rebelled in heaven and lost to Michael and the Faithful Angels, went into a sleep in which they dreamed of being somewhere else. The thought only occurred to them for a single moment that they could leave on their own and do something different, but nothing really happened.

The Holy Spirit, the Voice for God, came to the rescue immediately and told them that they really did not separate themselves from God. Some of the Siblings did not accept the Holy Spirit's response and dreamed that they separated from each other and from the *One Son* to an unreal world where God could not find them.

The thought of feeling separate was not a good idea! They experienced *fear* for the first time. *They made up their own thought system, which was only a dream, an illusion, where nothing was real. God would not be there.* It would be like excluding God, for surely the Heavenly Father would not enter their dream.

As my cousin, Mike Assemani, who is also a student of "A Course in Miracles" related to us in a group discussion, that God would not suddenly interrupt the dream of his *One Son* (or Children) any more than a parent watching her child having a dream or even a nightmare. She would not shake a child wildly to wake up; she would, as a wise mother, very slowly allow the child to awaken without fear or shock.

That is precisely what God is doing with us. We can take all the time in the world to awaken. In this one lifetime or have many "exits and entrances" to finally awaken to the Reality that the thought of separation never did take place. We should be forever grateful to the Heavenly Father for sending the Holy Spirit and the Lord Jesus to enter our **dream** and assist us on our journey Home.

We will only return Home when we are ready. Most of us choose the long way.

Mother Teresa chose a short cut by removing all thoughts of separation and seeing Christ in every person. She kept joining and joining with her brothers and sisters on the street or in the hospital to the degree that she became one with Christ and was considered a living Saint to the whole world. She gave us a wonderful example to follow.

Yet, there are still many people living in the world today (Hindus, Arabs, Jews and Asians) who are not familiar with Jesus' **Birth** (Christmas) nor His **Death** (Easter). This is surprising to me, since there have been many popular movies about Jesus seen around the world, besides having the world wide Internet available on our computers.

CHAPTER 5

TODAY, SOME BIBLE SCHOLARS CHALLENGE THE RESURRECTION OF JESUS FROM THE DEAD

Bible Scholars today have differing opinions about the life and especially about the Resurrection of Jesus Christ from the dead. If the Resurrection is true, it has to be the most amazing event in Human History!

Was Christ really the Son of God? The following is a brief look at the life of Jesus and why it is not blind faith to believe in Him.

Christ lived in obscurity as a carpenter until He was thirty and then began a Public Ministry for three years. His life was destined to change the Course of Human History. The common people loved to listen to Him. "He taught as one Who had authority and not as their teachers of the Law". (Matthew 7:29).

It soon became apparent, however, that the Lord Jesus Christ was making shocking and startling statements about Himself. He began to identify Himself as far more than a remarkable Teacher or Prophet. He began to say clearly that God was His Father. He made His **identity** the focal point of His teaching.

The all-important question He put to His disciples was, "Who do you say I am?" When Peter answered and said, "You are the Christ, the Son of the living God" (Matthew 16:15-16), Jesus was not shocked, nor did He rebuke Peter. On the contrary, He commended him!

His hearers got the full impact of His words. The New Testament says: "The Jews tried all the harder to kill Him;

not only was He breaking the Sabbath, but He was even calling God His own Father, making Himself equal with God" (John 5:18).

On another occasion he said, "I and My Father are One." Immediately the Jewish Authorities wanted to stone Him! He asked them for which good work did they want to kill Him. They replied, "We are not stoning You for any of these but for *blasphemy*, because You, a mere man, claim to be God" (John 10:33). Jesus, completely unharmed, simply walked through the crowd who were intent on killing Him.

Jesus clearly claimed Attributes only reserved to Almighty God. When a paralyzed man was let down through the roof wanting to be healed by Him, He said, "Son, your sins are forgiven you." This caused a great reaction among the religious leaders, who said in their hearts, "Why does this fellow talk like that? He's blaspheming! Who can forgive sins but God alone?"

At the critical moment when His life was at stake, the high priest put the question to Him directly: "Are You the Christ, the Son of the Living God?"

"I am", said Jesus. "And you will see the Son of Man sitting at the right hand of the Almighty One and coming on the clouds of heaven."

The high priest tore his garment. "Why do we need any more witnesses?" he asked. "You have heard the blasphemy!" (Mark 14:61-64).

So close was His connection with God that the Lord Jesus likened a person's attitude to Himself with the person's attitude toward God. Thus, to know Jesus was to know God (John 8:19; 14:7). To see Him was to see God (John 12:45;

14:9). To believe in Him was to believe in God (John 12:44; 14:1). And to honor Him was to honor God (John 5:23).

THERE ARE FOUR OPTIONS AMONG BIBLE SCHOLARS CONCERNING THE RESURRECTION OF JESUS FROM THE DEAD:

The Lord Jesus Christ was either a **liar**, a **lunatic**, a **legend** or **spoke the Truth**.

(1) One possibility is that Jesus lied when He said He was the Son of God, and deliberately deceived His hearers to lend authority to His teaching. Few Biblical authorities, if any, seriously hold this position. All Bible Scholars agree that He was a great moral teacher.

(2) A kinder, though no less shocking possibility, is that He was sincere but self-deceived. However, as we look at the life of Christ, we see no evidence of the abnormality and imbalance we find

in a deranged person. Rather, He demonstrated the greatest composure under pressure.

(3) The third alternative is that all of the talk about His claiming to be God's Son is a *"legend"* and His enthusiastic followers, in the third and fourth centuries, put words into His mouth that He was the Son of God.

The *"legend theory"* has been significantly refuted by many discoveries of modern Archeology. These have conclusively shown that the four Gospels of Christ were written while many of His contemporaries were still alive.

Some time ago, Dr. William F. Albright, the world-famous Archaeologist (now retired from Johns Hopkins University), said that there was no reason to believe that any of the Gospels were written later than 70 A.D.

He also added that a mere legend about Christ to have gained the circulation and a huge impact on the people still alive while the Gospels were being preached without one shred of basis in fact, is incredible.

Putting this in modern times would be just as fantastic as if someone wrote a biography of the late John F. Kennedy. If the biography said Kennedy claimed to be God, was able to forgive people's sins and rose from the dead, such a story would be so wild it would never get off the ground and people would laugh at it because there are too many people still alive who knew President Kennedy. In the same way, the *"legend theory"* does not hold water in the light of the early date of the Gospel manuscripts.

(4) The only other alternative is that Jesus spoke the Truth and had the

credentials to back up His claim. He said, "Even though you do not believe Me, believe the evidence of the works that I do (the miracles), that you may learn and understand that the Father is in Me, and I in the Father" (John 10:38).

EVIDENCE FROM THE SINLESS LIFE OF JESUS

The caliber of Christ's life was such that He was able to challenge His enemies with the question, "Can any of you prove Me guilty of sin?" (John 8:46). He was met by silence, even though He addressed those who would have liked to point out some negative comments about His character.

We read of the temptations of Jesus, but we never hear of a confession of sin on His part. He never asked for forgiveness, though He told His followers to do so.

First, Jesus' lack of any sense of moral failure is astonishing in view of the fact that His life is completely contrary to the experience of the Saints and Mystics throughout history. The closer they were to God, the more overwhelmed they became with their own failure, corruption, and shortcomings.

It is also striking that John, Paul and Peter, all of whom were trained from earliest childhood to believe in the universality of sin, spoke of the sinlessness of Jesus Christ: "He committed no sin and no deceit was found in His mouth" (1 Peter 2:22).

Pilate, no friend of Jesus, said, "What evil has He done?" He implicitly recognized Christ's innocence.

The Roman centurion who witnessed the death of Christ at the Crucifixion said, "Surely He was the Son of God!" (Matthew. 27:54).

Second, Christ demonstrated a power over nature which could belong only to God, the Author of Miracles and Divine Forces.

He stilled a raging storm of wind and waves on the Sea of Galilee. In doing this He provoked from those in the boat the awestruck question, "Who is this? Even the wind and waves obey Him!" (Mark 4:41)

He turned water into wine, fed 5,000 people from five loaves and two fish, gave a grieving widow back her only son by raising him from the dead, and brought to life another dead child of a shattered father. To an old friend He said, "Lazarus, come forth!" and dramatically raised him from the dead. It is most significant that His enemies did not deny these miracles! *Rather, they tried to kill Him.* "If we let Him go on like this," they said, "everyone will believe in Him" (John 11:48).

Third, Jesus demonstrated the Creator's power over sickness and disease. He made the lame to walk, the dumb to speak and the blind to see. Some of His healings were of congenital problems that are not susceptible to psychosomatic healing.

The most outstanding cure was that of the blind man whose case is recorded in the Gospel of St. John, Chapter 9. Though the man was unable to answer his persistent questioners, his experience was enough to convince them. "One thing I do know. I was blind but now I see!" he declared. He was astounded that his friends didn't recognize this Healer as the Son of God. "Nobody has ever heard of opening the eyes of a man born blind," he said (John 9:25, 32). To him the evidence was obvious.

Fourth, Jesus' ultimate evidence to validate His claim to be the Son of God, was His Resurrection from the dead. Five times in the course of His life He predicted He would die. He also predicted that three days later He would rise from the dead and appear to His disciples.

Surely this was His greatest test. It was a claim that was easy to verify among those still living after the Crucifixion. Either the *Resurrection* happened or it did not.

Both friends and enemies of the Christian Faith have recognized the Resurrection of Christ to be the foundation stone of the Christian Faith. Paul, the great Apostle, wrote, "If Christ has not been raised, our preaching is useless and so is our Faith" (1 Corinthians 15:14). Paul rested his whole case on the bodily

Resurrection of Christ. Either He did rise from the dead or He did not. If He did, it was the most sensational event in all of Human History.

CHAPTER 6

GOD'S ETERNAL, UNIVERSAL AND UNCHANGEABLE LAWS

In the 1970s and 1980s, I learned about the Laws of God from my studies in Metaphysics. My studies included information about the *conscious*, *subconscious* and even a *super-conscious* mind. I used to teach "Mind Development and Stress Control" classes in which we compared the conscious mind to the tip of an iceberg. Very little was known by the conscious mind which learned through the faulty and limited senses of the body.

The subconscious and super-conscious mind, on the other hand, were like the huge portion of an iceberg, most of it hidden underneath the waters and holding an unlimited amount of knowledge and mystery within us. It was, and is, in contact with our Soul and Spirit. The Subconscious Mind also contains the memory of everything we have ever experienced and is the source of our imagination and creativity.

A brief but powerful example of *"A Course in Miracles"* can be found in the *Text*, the first of the three books. It states clearly to human beings on Planet Earth:

there are *three Universal, Eternal, and Unchangeable Laws of God:*

1.   Nothing Real can be threatened.

2.   Nothing unreal exists.

3.   Here in lies the Peace of God.

The first Law: **Nothing Real Can be Threatened** referred only to that which is Eternal. Whatever the Infinite and Eternal God creates is Eternal and can never be threatened. Everything else can be threatened and, therefore, does not exist to God, the Eternal and Heavenly Father.

God is Perfect and whatever God creates is Eternal and Perfect. This world and this universe is a poor imitation.

In the same way, when you, as a human, have a child, that child is going to be human. It would take after you, be like you, be gifted with your genes, DNA, similar abilities and have the same color of skin. Besides the bloodline, children often adopt the same religious and political beliefs of their parents, including a general attitude toward life.

What God creates would be like the Creator, but nothing we can see is like our Divine Creator. Our bodies are certainly not like God, since God does not have a body! God is Pure Spirit! If you recall, anything that changes or can be threatened is not Eternally Perfect and does not exist according to the Lord Jesus. It is unreal! The mind can only **dream** about such a world. We are living in the dream!

You cannot have complete light and complete darkness at the same time. The absence of light is darkness. Is darkness real? No! Darkness does not really exist. In the same way, *Fear* results when a Soul forgets or is unaware that the Light of the Holy Spirit - God's Voice in this world - is always within us.

If you have a correct understanding of what I have just said, you are probably one of the wisest persons on this planet. Very few people have come to understand that. It is not compromising! It means exactly what it says about the difference between what is Real and what is unreal.

Can you think of anything on this planet that cannot be threatened? I cannot! Everything on **Planet Earth** can be threatened and will some day die or disappear.

So **Planet Earth** is unreal! According to the Lord Jesus, *NOTHING UNREAL EXISTS.* This world is real to us, but not to Our Heavenly Father who merely sees some of His Children dreaming. What would be something *unreal* on this planet? *Everything!* That means everything your eyes can see...even **Planet Earth** itself! Only what is Changeless and Eternal comes from God and cannot be threatened. There is nothing like that on this planet, including this entire physical universe.

Even thinking for a single moment that we have a life apart from God is absolutely impossible. If we share in God's Life and share in God's Love, our place in the Kingdom of God will never change. Although we are caught in the **dream**, there is nothing to fear. The *Message of Jesus* says: "God's Love sustains me and there is nothing to be afraid of."

When the Course uses the word Love, it means Unconditional Love, the kind of Love that has no conditions.

If love or marriage is based on certain conditions: **desperately** needing someone, or a strong **desire** *just to be* with someone, it may not last long and fear would result. When someone says I am doing this for you, because I love you, that is fine! If, however, their mind is harboring the thought "but don't forget that you owe me." That condition is called **love or generosity with a hook!** Again, the result is fear and often anger!

It's the same thing that happens at Christmas time. If someone gives you a gift but expects a gift in return, it is just another way of using or exploiting someone, regardless of whether it is a relative or a friend. True Love wants nothing in return. There is no need to fear or to be upset if you offer a gift that is not given in return.

Lately on television, they have been showing a group of volunteers who will rebuild a home for a poor family. Other volunteer groups help when there is a foreclosure on a recently purchased home. This is true generosity!

In God's Eternal Kingdom, there is no need to experience separation or fear. We cannot die, since we are God's Eternal Creation.

What kind of a planet are we living on? It is quite the opposite of God's Eternal Kingdom! We must do whatever we can just to survive! We, as humans, eat other living things. Plants are alive and everyone eats plants. Human beings eat animals. We are just eating whatever we can to stay alive on **Planet Earth**.

These conditions cannot come from God. If God created a flower, that flower can never die. It would be Eternal, Perfect, always beautiful in bloom and give off a wonderful aroma. An animal created by God would have Eternal Life and by sharing in God's Life can never be slaughtered for food. It would be Eternally Real and never threatened.

Look around you. Everything in your house can be threatened. I am sure that whatever your eyes see in your home or in the world will change or die. Even the trees! Are they permanent? Hardly! They change leaves every season and appear to die every winter in the north. I have just recently been informed that carpenter ants are now killing trees as well. That was news to me.

Nothing here is invincible. You can melt anything down, including gold, metal, rock and glass. Anything in this world can change. So none of this is Real! Nothing unreal exists, says the Son of God. In keeping with the Message of Jesus in 1965: *This world does not exist to our Creator and Heavenly Father!* To an Infinite God, some of His Children are still **dreaming** of leaving His Eternal Kingdom.

You might say: "Well I'm here! Those Siblings may not be here, but I'm here."

Yes, you are here *experiencing* life, but only in the **dream** made by the

collective _One Son God created._ God
sees us only as One Son!

None of us are here individually and
separate from each other. We may not be
aware of it, but our Spirit and our Mind
are forever _united as_ **one** in God's Mind.
In the dream, **Planet Earth** seems to be
real and we appear to be separated.

Actually, if we remember that we are
all Siblings in the _One Son_, it would be
the only Divine Creation on **Planet
Earth.**

**"The Kingdom of Heaven is within
you"**, Jesus said. But nothing around us
is created in the Image and Likeness of
God. Nothing! We cannot name a single
thing which our eyes see that is created
in God's Image, even the human body.
So, what is our conclusion? We think we
are here but we are really in God's
Kingdom **_dreaming_** that we are here. What

makes it seem possible are two gifts God gave us: a **Free Will** and a **split-mind**. Having a Free Will means that we can freely imagine being separate from God and from each other. A **split-mind** allows a part of our mind to be **asleep** in the Eternal Kingdom of God and to **dream** that we are separate from our Creator and from each other.

Our bodies seem to prove that we are really here and that we are separate from one another, but *our bodies are not real* since the human body is extremely fragile and very easily threatened. (The Son of God maintained that what can be threatened does not exist to the Heavenly Father!)

CHAPTER 7

WHAT IS THE EGO AND
ITS UNREAL WORLD?

I do not wish to go too deeply into this, but it is necessary to say something about the ego. **The ego is** *simply a* **thought** *of separation*, a belief that we are separate from God.

The Truth is that it would be absolutely impossible for God's Creation of the *One Son* before **time** began to be separate from God's Eternal Kingdom, even for a moment. The Holy Spirit made that clear when some of God's Children seriously thought of being elsewhere.

Quoting, in part, from Jesus' Message, "the ego is simply an idea that things could happen to the Children of God without their will and without the Will of our Creator."

This is a mad revolt and an insane idea which we have enshrined upon our altars and which we worship. **The body of Jesus in the dream was also part of the dream! Jesus now lives outside of time and space.** He truly is a Spiritual Being and the Eternal Son of God.

The Holy Spirit was unaware of the ego. It did not attack it. It merely cannot conceive of it at all. Yet, the *very* **thought** of possibly leaving God's Kingdom upset the entire Sonship, but it was only a **desire** to leave.

From True Knowledge and the correct Belief about our origin, no thoughts exist apart from God, because God and His Creation are *one* and can never be separated.

Unfortunately, most people on **Planet Earth** believe in the **dream** that all of us are separate from each other. That means that we experience division and conflict in our whole way of life. This is the ego's world and it is highly competitive. There are always opposites: we and they, you and I, our team against their team, our country against their country, our village against their village, etc.

This situation breeds continual **conflict** between two powerful forces ...and, eventually, with God. There is always a winner and a loser. The winners are very happy for the moment and the losers are unhappy, feeling hopeless and possibly crying even if they play Professional Basketball or Football.

I am writing this part of my book on Sunday, the third of February, 2008 just before the Super Bowl begins. There is going to be a winner and a loser between the Patriots and the Giants in Glendale,

Arizona. If you heard the game, you know that the New York Giants were celebrating late into the night. Some professional players are laughing and some are crying!

Remember, that *as God's One Son, called the Christ, we have an unlimited number of Siblings. The Heavenly Father sees only One Son here on* **Planet Earth** *and throughout the physical Universe although we believe we are separate.*

Planet Earth appears to be real because our conscious minds, being very limited, believe as Truth what we see, read or hear. **This leads to a world of illusions,** a world which needs constant defense precisely because it is unreal.

When any of us have been caught in the world of false thinking, we are trapped in the illusion. We cannot escape without help, because it is like being in quicksand. Everything our senses show us is also helpless and merely a witness to the illusion.

God has provided the **Answer** and the way to get out of this mess. We can be awakened with the aid of True and Divine Helpers. The Holy Spirit, in union with the Lord Jesus, mediate between God's World and this one. They can do this because they know the Truth. They also recognize our illusions without believing in them. They can help us escape from the dream world by teaching us how to reverse our thinking and to be given a second chance to learn from our mistakes.

"A Course in Miracles" refers to the **illusion** as the ***DETOUR INTO FEAR***: believing that we can change or distort what God has created and be our own creator.

None of these foolish ideas existed before the thought of separation, nor do they actually exist now. **The thought of an ego world is insane!** It believes in separation which is impossible and with false pride, even thinks it has achieved victory over God the Creator.

The program of "A Course in Miracles" is designed and carefully conceived to take a student of the Course, step by step, to a theoretical and practical level of understanding the Truth. The Course emphasizes *application* rather than *theory* and *experience* rather than *theology.* It specifically states that "a universal theology is impossible (since every religion has its own theology), but a universal experience is not only possible (life, work, family, sickness and death) but necessary." (Manual, p. 77)

Although Christian in statement, the Course deals with Universal Spiritual Themes. It emphasizes that it is but one version on the universal path that brings us closer to God. There are many other ways to establish an intimate relationship with God. Each one differs from one another only *in form*, but they all lead to God in the end. That is why the Message of Jesus is called "*A Course in Miracles*" and not "*The Course in Miracles*".

Mother Teresa, for example, was a Catholic Nun, attended daily Mass, said the Rosary each day and never studied "A Course in Miracles". Yet, in answer to Helen Schucman's question who could possibly live such a Course, Jesus told Helen that Mother Teresa lived it.

"*A Course in Miracles*" is considered the very heart of Jesus' Message given in 1965.

Since the **TEXT** is largely theoretical and describes in profound Wisdom the Concepts of the Course, one would almost need a dedicated group of people to study the TEXT together. The second book is called the **WORKBOOK.** It consists of lessons, one for each day of the year and helps to make the Text more understandable.

Although the Workbook consists of 365 lessons, one for each day of the year, it is not necessary, however, to take a lesson each day. The practical nature of the Workbook is underscored by the introduction to its lessons, which emphasize having **experience** through **application,** rather than a previous commitment to a spiritual goal.

Concerning the Workbook, "Remember only this; you need not believe the ideas, you need not accept them, and you need not even welcome them. Some of them you may even resist. None of this will matter or decrease their efficacy. But do not allow yourself to make exceptions in applying the ideas the *Workbook* contains and whatever your reactions to the ideas may be, use them. Nothing more is required." (Workbook, p. 2)

The last book written was the **MANUAL FOR TEACHERS**, which provides answers to some of the more likely questions a Teacher of the Course may be asked.

CHAPTER 8

THIS IS HOW
"A COURSE IN MIRACLES"
BEGINS

It describes the difference between what is Real and what is unreal. Divine Knowledge is Absolute Truth, subject to God's Eternal Laws and can never be threatened. It applies to everything that God created before there was time and space. It is outside of the realm of learning, has no opposite, no beginning and no end. It merely is! In the same way, the perfect definition of God would be: **God is!**

"A Course in Miracles" changes old and traditional words with a new understanding...words, such as: *sin, guilt, ego, salvation, eternity,*

judgement, holy instant, holiness and knowledge.

A more comprehensive meaning is also given to words like *Holy Spirit, love, creation, dream, God, fear, mind, the real world, Son of God and time.*

I studied "A Course in Miracles" with a group of friends. We were all very focused and dedicated to comprehend "A Course in Miracles", but even with our best intentions, there seemed to be some ideas and concepts we had trouble understanding.

Our world, called **Planet Earth**, is a world of *time, change* with constant *beginnings* and *endings*. It is based on ***interpretation***, not on *facts*. It is a world of birth and death, founded on a *negative belief system, including sin, guilt, anger and fear.* There are many fears! Some are undeniable **real fears** that there may be an earthquake or a tornado destroying one's home. These are facts which seem to be happening everywhere lately throughout the world.

Also, our world is becoming unsafe with our **protective OZONE layer getting thinner** over Australia, Antarctica and other areas in the world.

Many people are concerned that **Planet Earth** is getting to be overpopulated. They question whether there may be enough food or space for millions more living in our future.

Every family has the undeniable fear of some day losing their parents, siblings or friends through death. Such fears are experienced everywhere on the Earth. *In the Kingdom of God, or the Real World, such fears are not possible.*

How can we be sure of the difference between the Holy Spirit and the ego? It is very easy to tell the difference! The Holy Spirit always moves you to unite, whereas the ego wants you to separate. There are some people who want to kill other people, punish other people, despise other people with a different color of skin or detest those who worship differently.

These people believe you are there and I am here. They believe in right or wrong, good or bad, up and down, negative and positive. They are all listening to the voice of the ego. People that want revenge: "that person offended me, offended my family, offended my religion, I will kill him." That is straight from the heart of the ego.

SPECIAL RELATIONSHIPS of the world eventually become destructive, selfish and dominated by the ego or false image of who we really are. Yet, with the help of the Holy Spirit these relationships can become the holiest experiences on Earth - the miracles that point the way toward Heaven. The world uses its special relationships as a final weapon and as a false demonstration of being separate. The Holy Spirit offers a better option.

When we are ready to make our transition from this world and experience death, the Holy Spirit transforms our *holy relationships* into perfect lessons of forgiveness, and if we have lived according to the Divine Testimony of the Lord Jesus, we will experience a most exciting and unbelievable awakening from this unreal world.

Each relationship is an opportunity to let our minds be healed and our errors corrected. Each relationship is another chance to forgive oneself by forgiving another. In addition, each one becomes still another invitation by the Holy Spirit to remember our *oneness* in and with God.

Perception, or looking at an unreal world, is a function of the *body* and therefore represents a limit of *true awareness*. Perception sees through the body's eyes and hears through the body's ears. The result is a limited response which the body makes. The body appears to be largely self-motivated and independent; however, the body actually responds only to the intentions of the *mind*.

The **mind** is everything! If the mind wants to use the body for attack in any form, it becomes a victim with sickness, aging and decay. If the mind accepts God's Voice through Holy Spirit instead, it becomes a useful way of communicating with others. Everything in this world, being an illusion, is neutral. Whether it is used for the goals of the ego or the oneness in the Holy Spirit depends entirely on what the *mind wants*.

The opposite of seeing through the body's eyes is the **Vision of Christ** which reflects strength rather than weakness, unity rather than separation and love rather than fear. The opposite of hearing through the body's ears is communication through the Voice for God, the Holy Spirit, which abides in each of us.

His Voice seems distant and difficult to hear because the ego, which speaks for the little, insecure and separated self, seems to be much louder in this unreal world. This is the opposite of what it should be. The Holy Spirit speaks to us with unmistakable clarity and overwhelming appeal. Any person who does not choose to identify with the body will accept joyously the Vision of Christ in a glad exchange for the weak and miserable image of oneself as separate from the *One Son* or Children Created by God.

The point is to identify with your Spirit which is open to the Holy Spirit and not with your physical body which is unreliable, will get sick and die.

CHRIST'S VISION is the Holy Spirit's gift, which is God's alternative to the illusion of separation and to the false belief in the reality of sin, guilt and death. **Christ's Vision** is the correction for all the errors of our mind, helping us to see **that all is one.** There are no opposites from the Divine point of view.

Planet Earth happens to be filled with apparent opposites; that is why God could not have created it. **God is *one*** **and the Creation of the One Son is Eternal and forever in God's Kingdom.** The *Vision* or the *Light of Christ* unveils the thought system that results from True Knowledge, making a return to God with our Mind and Spirit not only possible, but inevitable.

Sin, sickness and attack are seen as *errors of the Mind*, calling for a remedy through gentleness and love. Defenses are laid aside, because where there is no attack, there is no need for defense. Our Siblings' needs become our own, because they are making the journey with us as we go to God. Without us they would lose their way. Without them we could never find our own.

There was *one single instant or moment long before time began, when some of our Siblings* in God's One Son had *a dream* or *illusion* of leaving God's

Kingdom. **The thought of leaving** God's Kingdom lasted a fraction of a second. *The Holy Spirit was immediately sent to tell them they were not able to leave!* Nothing existed outside of God's Eternal Kingdom. In spite of what the Holy Spirit said, certain defiant Siblings still insisted on leaving and other Siblings tried to stop them. This **conflict** resulted in the making of an unreal universe and a place to hide! Since it was only a **dream** or an **illusion**, God would not be there!

This unreal universe was a good hiding place, living in a world of *time* and space. A very small portion of this unreal universe was **Planet Earth...** the place where we live!

If we were experiencing Eternal Happiness in the Eternal Kingdom of Almighty God, why would anyone want to leave?

Good question!

A crazy, mad idea occurred to God's infinite number of Children. Since the Christ (God's *One Son* and Creation) shared in the Power of Almighty God, **THE THOUGHT** of some of God's Children being their own creator and leaving Heaven **WAS ONLY AN IDEA.**

It was not possible, since nothing existed outside of God's Kingdom. When the Holy Spirit reminded them no one could actually leave, some of our Siblings did not laugh, nor did they realize that the thought of leaving was such a silly idea! Instead, they became serious about certain negative thoughts right in the Eternal State of Heaven! They wanted to usurp and seize the very Power of God, their Divine Creator...a desire which was impossible, of course!

The only way any of them could leave the Eternal Kingdom of Heaven would be if part of their minds were asleep and they had a **dream** or an **illusion** of leaving.

Planet Earth is part of that dream. The years, days and hours are all unreal. We experience life in this dream. We sleep and dream every night. The difference is that living *this dream* on **Planet Earth** lasts a *lifetime* since it was made by the *collective mind* of God's Son, an abuse of Divine Power.

As individuals separate and alone, the unreal universe appears to be much greater than any one of us. Jesus was an exception; He performed *miracles*, because He knew it was not Real.

"A Course in Miracles" says that the world we see is not real, but reflects our own personal point of view. If we usually read the newspapers or watch

television and imagine a world of fear with frightening thoughts of being mugged or attacked, we will conclude that the world is full of evil, destruction, crime, hatred and despair. All this we must learn to forgive, not only because we are being a "good neighbor", but because what we are seeing is simply not true.

The marvelous **Vision of Christ** sees all things from another point of view, reflecting on the thought system that results from Divine Knowledge. What was regarded as injustice done to one another, now becomes a call for help and unity. Sin, sickness, guilt, fear and attack are seen as a false belief in need of gentleness and love. Defenses are laid aside, because where there is no attack, there is no need for a defense.

"This Course is a beginning, not an end. No more specific lessons are assigned, for there is no more need of them. Henceforth, hear but the Voice for God. He will direct your efforts, telling you exactly what to do, how to direct your mind and when to come to Him in silence, asking for His sure direction and His certain Word." (Workbook, p. 487).

Knowledge is Truth, under one law, the Law of Love, or God. DIVINE TRUTH IS UNCHANGEABLE AND ETERNAL. God's Truth may or may not be recognized in this world, yet His Truth applies to everything that God created and what God creates is Eternally Real. It is beyond learning, because it is beyond time and space. In fact, God has no opposite. There is no beginning and no end, just as a perfect definition of God would be: **God is!**

From my background and experience I see some problems connected with the Course. My concern with ideas about what is Real and unreal, and the difference between what is made and what is created. I also have personal problems with what is called reincarnation and karma. In God's World, they do not exist!

CHAPTER 9

WHO WAS
WILLIAM SHAKESPEARE?

Shakespeare had much to say about life on **Planet Earth**. Shakespeare is considered by most authors and most people in general as the greatest writer of all time. I wanted to know more about him, so I did a little research on his life. Who was he? Where did he come from? I believe, among other things about him, that Shakespeare was well ahead of his time when he said that **"All the world is a stage and all the men and women merely players; they have their exits and their entrances."** It's quite true! Each one of us has a different role in life and that role is helping us to become a fuller human being, even if we have just one brief experience on **PLANET EARTH.**

Each life here is an experience and it has its purpose. Let's say you are 5 years old and you die, never achieving the goals of an adult. Or let's say you were stillborn or actually aborted **you may have chosen those conditions which perhaps accomplished an important lesson for your parents and others to learn.** Maybe the sacrifice you made in giving up a life means you achieved considerable, spiritual progress in the sight of God.

Others, as Shakespeare continues to say, will experience a complete lifetime of seven levels of living, beginning with **birth** and ending with old age and **death.**

For all his fame and celebration, William Shakespeare remains a mysterious figure with regards to his personal history. There are just two primary sources for information on this great writer: various legal and church documents that have survived from Elizabethan times. Naturally, there are many gaps in this body of information, which tells us little about Shakespeare the man.

William Shakespeare was born in Stratford-upon-Avon, allegedly on April 23, 1564. Young William was born of John Shakespeare, a glover and leather merchant and Mary Arden, a landed local heiress. William, according to the church register, was the third of eight children in the Shakespeare household - three of whom died in childhood. John Shakespeare had remarkable success as a merchant, alderman and high bailiff of Stratford during William Shakespeare's childhood. Later, his father's fortune declined in the late 1570s.

There are some concerns regarding William's education. Some biographers think that Shakespeare attended the free grammar school in Stratford, which, at the time, had a reputation of rivalry with Eton School. It is believed that Shakespeare had a good background of Latin and Classical Greek. His father, being a Stratford official, was granted a waiver of tuition for the education of his son William, who never attended a University. This generated a lot of debate about his authorship.

Shakespeare married Anne Hathaway on November 28, 1582. William was 18 at the time and Anne was 26 and pregnant. They had a daughter, Susanna and later, twins: Hamnet and Judith. They were all baptized at Holy Trinity Church in Stratford. For the next seven years, Shakespeare disappeared from all records, then he finally turned up again in London around 1588 and began to establish himself as an actor and playwright. Shakespeare's success is obvious when compared with other playwrights of his time. In fact, his company was the most successful in London. He even had plays published and sold in special editions to the more literate of his audiences.

Never before had a playwright enjoyed such notoriety to see his works published and sold as popular literature in the midst of his career. In addition, Shakespeare's share in the ownership of a theatrical company and in the **"Globe"** made him as much an entrepreneur as an artist. Although Shakespeare may not have been considered wealthy by London standards, his success allowed him to purchase a new house and retire in comfort to Stratford in 1611.

William Shakespeare's legacy is a body of work that will never again be equaled in Western Civilization. His words have endured for 400 years and still reach across the centuries as powerfully as ever. Even in death, he leaves a final piece of verse as his epitaph:

"Good friend, for Jesus' sake forbeare to dig the dust enclosed here. Blessed be the man that spares these stones, and cursed be he that moves my bones."

Along with Shakespeare, let me just say that *we are all on stage* acting in a play. We are living in the world of the ego and the word *ego* is similar to the word *Devil* since its purpose is the same: to make us think we are separate from God and from each other. We are really not here as separate individuals. If we took the ego's world, which is our whole universe, including our earth and see it as *time and space, a scientist might estimate it to be 15 to 20 billion years, even though it is not real.* In Reality, it is merely an **illusion**.

Other modern authors go a step further than a role on Shakespeare's World Stage in which everyone has their exits and their entrances. They say that the *exits and entrances* on Shakespeare's Stage may be a desire to gather more experiences in the world of *time* and *space*. Our Immortal Spirit may desire to have the experience of being a man, a woman, a doctor, a thief, a princess, a soldier, etc. It really doesn't matter. Nothing happens! Part of our mind is asleep with the **split-mind**, and we can only **dream** about leaving God's Eternal Kingdom.

Our Spirit, our Soul and our Subconscious Mind are Eternal, but the physical body is only a temporary vehicle in the **dream**. The book **"Disappearance of the Universe"**, the

Cayce Readings and the many other Teachers in Metaphysics all agree that our role is to **discover** and **remember** who we are and why we are on **Planet Earth.**

We are on a small planet which has no effect whatsoever on our galaxy, a massive ensemble of over two hundred billion stars orbiting about a common center. Astronomers estimate that there are about 125 billion Galaxies in the Universe. All the stars visible to the unaided eye from Earth belong to **The Milky Way, Planet Earth's** galaxy.

Our solar system is just one star in this galaxy with more than 200 billion other stars. Our sun is just an average star and **Planet Earth** is just an average planet among billions of other planets.

The above picture is an estimated view of the Milky Way Galaxy, thanks to the imagination and amazing pictures of outer space by the Hubble Telescope.

This picture makes it even clearer, showing the enormous distance in Light Years that **Planet Earth** is from the center of the dynamic and continual activity of The Milky Way.

Our sun and its solar system are trillions of miles away from the other star systems. Included is a lonely and tiny **Planet Earth** which has no apparent effect on our huge galaxy. That is why we do not see many stars or planets at night. At the Central Bulge in the picture above, there must be an abundance of activity since the stars systems with their satellites and moons are very close to one another. Night time does not exist there.

How did we end up on this tiny, insignificant **Planet Earth,** a little dot in a huge physical universe...and why? That is precisely why I am writing this book. After reading this book, I hope you will have a better understanding of where we came from and why we are on **Planet Earth.**

CHAPTER 10

EINSTEIN:
SCIENCE, MATH AND RELIGION

Einstein, as a genius, is a household word throughout the world. I felt it important to know what Einstein believed about God, our Heavenly Father. I discovered that he had his own set of beliefs, which is not surprising.

There was an article in the April 16, 2007 Time Magazine on the life of Albert Einstein. As a young man, Einstein rejected his parents' Jewish traditional beliefs. They were simple tradesmen and peddlers who made a modest living in several villages of Swabia in Southwestern Germany. Their family history went as far back as two hundred years before young Einstein was born.

When Einstein was just 10 years old, he went to a Catholic School. There were 70 students in his class and he was the only Jew. He took classes in the Catholic Faith, but he suddenly had a strong desire to return to his Jewish background. He ate no pork, kept kosher and obeyed the laws concerning the Sabbath. He even composed his own hymns, which he sang to himself as he walked home from school. The Einstein family hosted a 21 year old medical student, called Max Talmud, who came from a poor family, to share a Sabbath meal with them every week.

Max brought books on science and math to the 10 year old, Albert Einstein. Young Albert Einstein was especially interested in the 21 volumes written by Aaron Bernstein, whose books stressed the interrelations between Biology and Physics. Einstein was driven with such passion in his studies that he was already shaping his destiny of some day being acknowledged as a great scientist and genius. Max said that Einstein learned so fast that he was no longer able to continue as his teacher.

Max and young Albert Einstein used to read and discuss scientific and philosophical works. At the age of 12, Albert got to know the "Holy Geometry" book which impressed him very much. With the aid of a teacher and a Rabbi, Einstein prepared to become a "Bar-Mizwa" - a full member of the Jewish Community. However, he did not go to his "Bar-Mizwa", because he started to become a freethinker.

Due to reasons at work Hermann Einstein, the father of Albert Einstein, moved to Italy with his wife and daughter. Albert Einstein stayed with relatives in Munich, Germany to finish school. He left the Luitpold-Gymnasium (University) without a degree in

December and followed his family to Milan.

Einstein did not pass the entrance examination to the Polytechnic (later called the Swiss Technical college) in Zurich. He attended the Trade Department of the school in Aarau to make up for failing to submit to the school examination and evaluation. Meantime, he lived with the family of one of his teachers, Jost Winteler. Einstein wrote his first scientific work, but it was not published.

At the age of 17, Einstein gave up his German Citizenship and succeeded in being qualified for the University entrance this time. He wanted to achieve a certificate in Mathematics and Physics. Two years later, he was granted a Swiss Citizenship.

His first scientific work was the "Annals of Physics". He worked at the

"Patent Office" in Bern and transformed the basics of Physics around 1900. One of his works On "The Electrodynamics of Moving Bodies" contained the Special Theory of Relativity. In another work, he gave the world his most famous formula: $E = MC^2$.

The following year he was awarded a Doctorate at the University of Berlin. In 1909, Einstein was awarded an honorary Doctorate at the University of Geneva with more Doctorates and Awards to follow. He became a full Professor at the German University of Prague. In 1913, he was offered a membership in the famous Prussian Academy of Sciences. His articles on the Special and General Theory of Relativity and the Quantum Theory added to his fame.

In 1929, when Einstein was 50 years old and known as a household name almost everywhere in the world, he was interviewed by George Sylvester Viereck. Viereck did not waste any time with his questions: Are you a German or a Jew?"

Einstein replied: "It's possible to be both; nationalism is an infantile disease, the measles of mankind."

He was then asked to what extent was he influenced by Christianity.

Einstein said in response: "As a child, I received instructions both in the Bible and in the Talmud. I am a Jew, but I am enthralled by the luminous figure of the Nazarene."

"You accept the historical existence of Jesus?"

"Unquestionably! No one can read the Gospels without feeling the actual presence of Jesus. His personality pulsates in every word. No myth is filled with such a life."

"Do you believe in God?"

Einstein replied: "I am not an atheist! I believe in a God Who reveals Himself in the Lawful Harmony of all that exists, but not in a God Who concerns Himself with the fate and the doings of mankind."

Copernicus and Galileo are examples of other great minds who were rejected for their beliefs about the Universe, but were later proven to be correct. And there were others.

In Jesus' recent Message called *"A Course in Miracles"*, He says the same thing: God the Father does not enter this world which is a ***dream*** of His One Son (composed of an infinite number of Children), but sent the Holy Spirit and the Lord Jesus to Planet Earth in order to help us to awaken from the dream and remember who we are. In the Eternal and

Real Kingdom of God, the Heavenly Father created all that is Real and Eternal, and keeps the galaxies and star systems of His Universe in Lawful Harmony.

Even Planet Earth, an unreal world of illusion, must also obey God's Eternal Laws. If not, in this imperfect dream of a universe, Planet Earth could have been destroyed by a comet or another planet millions of years ago.

These little dots are separate
galaxies. There are hundreds of
billions of galaxies scattered
throughout the universe. Each galaxy is
composed of at least 200 billion star
systems. The stars and planets in the
unreal and temporary universe are almost
infinite in number.

CHAPTER 11

PLANET EARTH IS LIKE A BUSY AIRPORT WITH SOULS DREAMING OF EXPERIENCE

I compare the Planet Earth to a busy airport, with about 7,000 people dying every day in the United States alone and more than 7,000 being born in the United States every day of the year. Since the United States is only a small area of the entire **Planet Earth,** there are literally millions of Souls who die daily and millions more who are born every day throughout the world.

Michigan recorded 86,900 deaths in 2005, more than 1700 deaths than occurred in the previous year. *Heart disease* and *stroke* - the no. 1 and no. 3 killers - caused fewer deaths in 2005 than in 2004. But the no. 2 killer, *cancer*, rose to about 660,000 from 554,000.

Life expectancy is now almost 78 years in the United States.

You may wonder where all these souls are coming from as they enter Planet Earth. Remember, in God's *One Son, called the Christ*, we have millions of Siblings. We are all God's Children! In fact, the number of Siblings is infinite!

Almost on cue, the very same day that I was writing this page - September 13, 2007 - I read in the *Detroit Free Press* that there was a report released by the National Center for Health Statistics. The article said that the number of people in America who died in the past year was nearly 2,500,000. The number of births usually is greater in number than deaths. That is why the population in the United States and almost every country in the world is growing year by year. There are 6.7 billion people on the Earth today. Every day, millions of souls are making their journey to Planet Earth through birth and millions are leaving Planet Earth every day through death.

Where do these souls come from? The conflict between some of God's Children who were determined to leave the Eternal Kingdom of Heaven and other Siblings who tried to persuade them to stay, ended in a conflict that made a place to hide from God for fear of being punished.

Since it was only a *dream*, allowing part of their minds to be asleep, it was not real and God would not enter His Sons' dream or illusion. That *dream* turned out to be a universe that was not real...a very faulty and imperfect imitation of God's Eternal Kingdom.

Planet Earth is a part of that unreal universe.

Planet Earth may not be real, but the souls in this *dream* are having *genuine experiences* that can be brief moments of happiness or times of doubts and fears that can be terribly painful. Everything is so uncertain here: the daily weather report is often wrong, some of the articles written in our Newspapers are not always based on fact and we cannot believe everything we see on the computer. The News on the computer is live, up-to-date and worldwide, but such information can be very harmful in the wrong hands.

So let me just say, in keeping with Shakespeare's view of life, that the world is a stage and all the men and women have their exits and entrances. *We are all on stage acting out in a play here*. Mind you, it is not real, it is only a play. Sometimes we happened to be in the same play, each of us having different roles in the same play! While we are in the play, we made up hours, days and years to keep track of our imagined time here, like punching your card in the time-clock at work.

Does time exist as billions of years since the "Big Bang"?

The answer is no! Time does not exist even though it seems to govern every moment of our lives. I frequently look at the watch on my wrist. I am always conscious of time even though I am homebound and a shut-in because of ill health. Some people, who still have jobs and do not live close to their work place, have to drive through heavy traffic every day, sometimes with the sun in their face, to clock in and report for work.

In spite of all that I just wrote above, Jesus' message in "A Course in Miracles" states clearly **that there is no such thing as time!**

Even though scientists say that the universe was created between 10 and 20 billion years ago from a cosmic explosion that hurled Galaxies, star systems, comets and planets in all directions. This theory also explains why distant Galaxies are still traveling away from us at great speeds. The Big Bang Theory received its strongest confirmation when the radiation(the glow left over from the explosion itself) was discovered in 1964 by Arno Penzias and Robert Wilson, who later won the Nobel Prize for this discovery.

***TIME* HERE IS JUST PART OF THE ILLUSION. IT IS NOT REAL!** I have a wrist watch and I am frequently looking at it. On Planet Earth, we all live by the clock. Time seems to govern our very existence. We think of time as moving on in days and years: we are born into a world of *time* as a young child, soon to become a teenager, then an adult and finally our hair starts getting grey and Society calls us Seniors; then comes retirement, subjecting us to sickness and death.

Again, I am saying that there is no such thing as time because Eternity and God's Eternal Kingdom came first and it removes and eliminates even the possibility of time.

Even though we seem to be passing through different periods of time, **everything is happening all at once.** It also means that different moments of time are the exact same moment, filled with different scenery. **Time is one, single all-encompassing instant.** It is hard to believe in this illusion, but this current moment is the same moment as when there were giant animals like the dinosaurs roaming the earth or when Jesus was born on the first Christmas.

Our minds here are like the light of a movie projector, seeing through different frames of film, one frame at a time. It is just a mental trick we are playing. The fact is that we are experiencing these different frames of film all at once - in one instant - according to Jesus' message of "A Course in Miracles", but it is impossible for our current minds to comprehend this.

Even more surprising is that the one single instant has already happened. It's over! We are now simply reliving memories of that instant.

No two people have the same role in the same play. Now these plays are going on all *at the same time*. Let's say that, in the dream, we were in a play in

the twelfth century or the nineteenth
century, those plays are going on *now*,
since this is all there is. There is no
past and there is no future in God's
Mind. It has to be *now*. I am now in
that play, I am now in this play, I am
now in another play, all going on at the
same time in the Eternal Now. Since we
have never left God's Eternal Kingdom
and can only *dream* that we did, there is
no such thing as **Time** or
Reincarnation... unless we believe that
this world is Real! And it is not!

We are all going through various
roles in each play by our own choice. We
came here to **experience** and to **remember**
who we are and why we are here. We have
forgotten that we are the Siblings of
God, Our Divine Creator and that we were
created in the Image and Likeness of
God, as *One Son*, which took place long
before there was any concept of male and
female.

Edgar Cayce, the world's greatest psychic of our time says that Jesus is the one who started many of the major religions in different parts of the world. Jesus so identified with the Christ (God's only Son and Creation) that he became the Christ... Jesus, the Christ.

We are really not here as individuals. If we took all of *time*, including all ancient history since the so-called Big Bang, what we call *time* is just one tiny, very tiny point on the grand scale of Reality. When people died 10, 20 or 50 years ago, we carry the sad memory in our hearts of their transition by death into the Spirit world. **TIME** is a trick of the mind and just another name for a **dream** or an **illusion**. To Almighty God, their deaths are happening right now. God lives in the *now* moment! To God there is no yesterday or tomorrow! I will repeat this fact as often as I can: **God *lives* in the Eternal Now.**

The present moment is like a window in which the Creator and His Child (you, myself and any of our Siblings) can remember being at Home again with Our Heavenly Father. Praying is very good, but our prayers are much more powerful when united with God in a *holy instant*.

CHAPTER 12

EACH OF US HAS TO DECIDE BETWEEN TWO OPPOSITE THOUGHT SYSTEMS AS A WAY OF LIFE

There are different levels of understanding in this world. You have a choice between two thought systems: One is *"God's Divine and Eternal Thought System"* and the other is *"The false and imperfect world of the ego."* The ego's thoughts, being a separate thought system based on illusion and separation, is a misuse of God's Power.

It is uncompromising! You have to choose between God's world and this imperfect, vicious world of the ego.

The Holy Spirit or the Lord Jesus, the Voice for God in this world, would say: "Father, forgive them for they know not what they do." We can get out of this mess, which the Church calls "the veil of tears", by following Their Divine Guidance.

In the realm of Truth and Knowledge, no thoughts exist apart from God, because God and His Creation are *one* and can never be separated. Unfortunately, most people on Planet Earth believe that all of us are separate from each other. That means that we experience division and conflict in our whole way of life. The result is continual conflict with each other...and, eventually, with God. Remember, that *as God's One Son, called the Christ, we have millions of Siblings. The Heavenly Father sees only One Son here on Planet Earth although we believe we are separate.*

Planet Earth appears to be real, because our conscious minds, being very limited, believe what we see, read about, hear about from others and feel through the body's senses. This leads to a world of illusions, a world which needs constant defense precisely because it is not real.

When any of us have been caught in the world of false thinking, we are trapped in the *dream*. We cannot escape without help, because it is like being in quicksand and everything our senses show us are also helpless and merely witnesses to the reality of the dream.

God has provided the *Answer* and the way to get out of this mess. We can be awakened with the aid of True and Divine Helpers. **It is the function of the Holy Spirit, in union with the Lord Jesus, to mediate between God's World and this one. They can do this because They know the Truth.** They also recognize our illusions without believing in them. Either the Holy Spirit or the Lord Jesus can help us escape from the dream world by teaching us how to reverse our thinking and to be given a second chance to learn from our mistakes.

The Course clarified for me why we are here from a Divine point of view. It is not just another opinion or guessing what the Truth may be. *I believe "A Course in Miracles"* is the Truth and a word-for-word Testimony of Our Lord Jesus Christ, the Son of God. It seems to be the only way Home and out of this mess.

The world we see and feel describes what is in our mind: our personal ideas, desires, wishes, fears, guilt, emotions and the complete *innocence* of not realizing that anything our eyes see is not Eternal and therefore not created by Almighty God.

Our minds are like a movie projector. The thoughts are inside of our minds and

we then project them outside of us to
see the kind of picture we expect to see
on the movie screen. What we see is an
unreal world which becomes our truth.
We make it true by our interpretation of
what it is we are seeing. If our minds
are filled with hateful and dangerous
ideas, we will see a world without hope,
a world invaded by anger, thoughts of
attack, the lack of Love, evil,
destruction, injustice, crime, envy and
despair. All this we must learn to
forgive, not because we are being a
loving or *good neighbor*, but because
Jesus states clearly that what we are
seeing outside of ourselves is simply
not True or Real.

Unfortunately, we have distorted the
world by our misunderstanding of what we
think is out there and our unreal
defenses. As we learn to recognize our
original and fundamental error in the
belief that we are separate from each

other and from our Creator, we also learn to look past these errors and to *forgive*. At the same time, we are forgiving ourselves and our distorted self-image in order to remember our True Self as Siblings in the *One Son* God created.

There are many ways to forgive and achieve the experience of Freedom. Maybe we can break down the process of forgiveness through three steps:

1. Recall your present unforgiving thought or perception about other people, remembering their faults, the problems you had with them, the pain they caused you and their vicious behavior toward you. You may be thinking of their other actions as immoral or sinful.

2. Dwell on some loving words that offer a new idea about them: Words of kindness, affection and letting go. The

Workbook (Lesson 161) of the Course suggests asking of him:

"Give me your blessing, holy Son of God. I would behold you with the eyes of Christ and see my perfect sinlessness in you."

3. This idea keeps us secure from anger and from fear. The request for a blessing should be used immediately if we are tempted to attack one of our Siblings and see in him the *symbol* of our fear. And we will see him suddenly *transformed* from enemy to savior; from the devil to Christ." These are the words of the Lord Jesus in His Message.

You can, therefore, listen to the prompting of the Holy Spirit or the imperfect urges of the ego. Nothing else exists. It is uncompromising!

CHAPTER 13

PROJECTION MAKES PERCEPTION

The world you see is what you gave it, nothing more than that. To you it is important and is a witness of your state of mind. "As man thinks, so does he perceive." **Perception is a result and not a cause.** Therefore, do not try to change the world, but rather *change your mind about the world*. Everything looked upon with the Vision of Christ is Healed and Holy. Otherwise, it would have no meaning...which amounts to chaos.

"A Course in Miracles" says that this is the only thing that you need do for expressing the Vision of Christ. Happiness, release from pain and the complete escape from sin will be yours. Say only this where the power of salvation lies:

"I am responsible for what I see.

I choose the feelings I experience, and I decide upon the goal I would achieve.

And everything that seems to happen to me I ask for and receive as I have asked."

Acknowledge that you have been mistaken and all effects of your mistakes will disappear. **It is impossible for anything harmful to happen to God's children against their will.** No accident or chance is possible within the Universe as God created it, outside of which is nothing.

Projection reminds us that our minds are like a movie projector. The thoughts are inside of our minds and we then project them outside of us to see the kind of picture we expect to see on the movie screen. What we perceive is an unreal world which becomes our truth. We make it true by our interpretation of what we are seeing. The world we see and feel describes what is in our mind: our personal ideas, desires, wishes, fears, guilt, emotions and the complete *innocence* of not realizing that anything our eyes see is not Eternal and, therefore, not created by Almighty God.

If our minds are filled with hateful and dangerous ideas, we will see a world without hope, a world invaded by anger, thoughts of attack, the lack of Love, evil, destruction, injustice, crime, envy and despair. All this we must learn to *forgive*, not because we are being a *loving* or *good* person, but because Jesus states clearly that what we are seeing outside of ourselves is simply not True or Real.

Unfortunately, we have distorted the world by our misunderstanding of what we think is out there and our unreal defenses. As we learn to recognize our original and fundamental error in the belief that we are separate from each other and from our Creator, we also learn to look past these errors and to *forgive*. At the same time, we are forgiving ourselves and our distorted self-image in order to remember our True Self as Siblings in the **One Son** God created.

Sin is defined as a "lack of love" (Text, p. 11). *Since Divine Love is all there is, sin in the sight of the Holy Spirit is not possible!* **Sin is a *mistake* to be corrected, rather than an *evil* to be punished.** It is not unusual for any one of us, at times, to feel unsafe and fearful, living in a world filled with anxiety and warfare (There are about 40 wars between countries or within a particular country at any given moment on the Earth). Sad to say, most people live by what may be called **THE SCARCITY PRINCIPLE** that governs the whole world of illusions. From a negative point of view, we seek in others what we feel is *scarce* or *lacking* in ourselves. There are certain cities, townships and villages fighting all the time in some countries, because *others* have a different color, belief system or culture. We can call them Wars, because they are severe conflicts causing injury and death.

If we sincerely believe that we are *separate individuals*, we usually care about one another in order to get something from the other person that is pleasing to ourselves. That, in fact, is generally what passes for *"love"* in the dream world. There can be no greater mistake than that, since *True Love* is incapable of asking for anything. True Love craves an intimacy with our Divine Creator and Heavenly Father...Jesus is a perfect example.

Only *minds* can really *join*. (Text, p. 356). It is, however, only at the level of the *Mind of Christ* that **True Union** is possible and has, in fact, never been lost. The Real Self in us that God created needs nothing. It is forever complete, safe, loved and loving. It seeks to *share* rather than to *take*; to *extend* rather than *project*. It has no needs and wants to join with others out of their mutual awareness of abundance.

God's Eternal Kingdom is forever Beautiful, Peaceful and Perfect in every way. Yet, somehow a *crazy, mad* idea occurred to God's Son, the Christ, (God's Children in which all of us are Siblings) that we could do something better. Some of our Siblings had the thought of leaving and exploring somewhere else and had to fight Michael, Jesus and the Faithful Ones. Like the angels who failed, so did the rebellious Children perceive a challenge they could not win.

I have come to believe, after studying "A Course in Miracles", nothing actually happened. The Holy Spirit, the Voice for God, immediately told them that they could not separate themselves from God. They did not accept the Holy Spirit's response, so they allowed a part of their minds to be asleep and dream of being elsewhere where God could not find them. Feeling separate from each other and from God, they experienced fear, sin and guilt. They made up their own thought system (the ego) which was not real. In fact, it was only a dream, an illusion, where nothing is real.

That is precisely what God is doing with us. We can take all the time in the world to awaken...right away, or take as long as we wish in order to finally awaken to Reality. The work of the Holy Spirit and the Lord Jesus is to enter your dream and assist you to return Home. We will only come Home when we are ready. we can return quickly or choose the long way Home.

You have been moved by the Holy Spirit. You were inspired to fulfill your life by marrying a certain person who was pre-arranged for you before you were born. The Holy Spirit simply reminds you of what you agreed to accomplish in this life. He often works in subtle ways setting up the conditions of how and where you would meet, allowing one thing to follow another and leading you both to your wedding vows.

Many Souls will continue to experience life in this unreal universe for many years to come, unless we are on the earth during an actual *Global Warming* in which the earth is no longer safe. The heat of the Sun or a stray comet or asteroid could penetrate our protective atmosphere. Millions would die all across the **Planet Earth**. In order to understand global warming, first, one must understand a natural process called **"The Greenhouse Effect"**.

Every day, the sun's rays are absorbed by the Earth and converted to heat. As the Earth cools down at night, it loses a lot of the heat that it has absorbed into outer space, thanks to the Earth's atmosphere and its essential mixture of gases. It is mainly nitrogen and oxygen, but it also contains methane (CH_4), carbon dioxide (CO_2), and nitrous oxide (N_2O). These three gases are able to absorb heat lost by the Earth and radiate it back to the Earth. This radiation is crucial for the survival of life on **Planet Earth.**

All three of these gases exist naturally. The problem is that the amount of carbon dioxide in the atmosphere has been steadily increasing. More heat is being radiated back to the Earth. This causes the temperature of the Earth to continue rising. Scientists maintain that a change of just a few degrees will drastically alter the planet.

Global Warming is a real issue! Since carbon dioxide is a product of the excessive and abundant use of fuels, such as gasoline and coal, carbon dioxide will continue to increase and some day may cause horrible floods and tidal waves all across the planet.

As we **project** a global warming and its horrible effects, we **perceive** the effect with the thinning of the ozone layer that protects **Planet Earth**.

CHAPTER 14

DOES TIME EXIST AS BILLIONS OF YEARS?

What we call *time* is just one tiny point on the grand scale of Eternity. Scientists consider time as the billions of years since the "Big Bang". From Jesus Message, known around the world as "A Course in Miracles" **TIME DOES NOT EXIST. IT IS ONLY A DREAM OR AN ILLUSION.**

When people died 20, 30 or 50 years ago, we experienced great sorrow at the lost of a loved one. Since God only exists in the *Eternal Now*, where *time* does not exist, and since God is the only True and Eternal Reality, our loved ones are passing over into the world of spirit right **now...** where clock-time does not exist. Will they remember us?

Of course. It just happened! There is no yesterday or tomorrow in God's World. **Everything is going on right now**... at this very moment. We think we are all separate from one another, but according to the Message of the Lord Jesus, the Son of God, we never left the Eternal Kingdom. In fact, He says the Truth is that *"WE ARE ON A JOURNEY WITHOUT DISTANCE TO A PLACE WE HAVE NEVER LEFT," which means that we are still in God's Kingdom.*

The **thought** of being separated from God was projected from our minds to prove that the ego is not insane or just a crazy idea. The belief in separation, however, seems to be everywhere on **Planet Earth** as if it were an absolute truth. We all have a feeling of being vulnerable. Nothing stays the same; everything we see is unstable. This certainly is not Heaven. What is Heaven like? If we were able to take the happiest moment or the most exciting event of our life and multiply it ten or twenty thousand times and lasting forever, it would only give us a vague and shadowy glimpse of what God's Eternal Heaven or Kingdom is like.

Forgiveness is the key word. Forgiving is our ticket to freedom. It's often easy to forgive someone else. Who is harder to forgive? Ourselves, of course! It's much harder to forgive oneself.

The now moment is very important to us on **Planet Earth, since it is *the only time*, like an open window,** in which we are able to communicate directly with God.

We came here with the opportunity to **experience** and to **remember** who we are. We have forgotten that ***we are the One***

Son (God's Children), created in the Image and Likeness of God. Along with Jesus, we are also the Sons and Daughters of Almighty God.

The origin of measuring TIME goes back to the **Sumerian** civilization around 2,000 BC. It was a system based on sixty: 60 seconds in a minute, 60 minutes in an hour - and a calendar with 360(60x6)days in a year(a few more days were added later.) The number twelve was also included: 12 hours of day and 12 hours of night, and 12 months in a year(with 12 being 1/5 of 60).

Ferdinand Magellan was sent by the King of Spain to sail around the world, proving that the earth was round and hopefully, to find new treasures for Spain. Magellan used 18 drinking glasses on each ship for the trip. One glass for each day. The passage at sea was marked by these **"bells"**. The Middle

Dutch word "klocke" and the Latin word "**clocca**" along with the French and German words all meant "**bell**". I believe that is the origin of the word "**clock**" for us in English.

Other civilizations used the **Sundial** to judge time. In monasteries, temples and churches, they used **incense sticks** and **Candles** to measure time across the globe. At sea, the **Hourglass** used the flow of sand to measure the flow of time.

Since 1967, the most accurate type of timekeeping today is the "**atomic clock**", which is *accurate to the second* in many thousands of years and which the International System of Measurements uses to help in correcting other timekeeping instruments.

Actually, the earliest recorded philosophy of time was spelled out by the **Egyptian Phathotep,** who lived around 2600 BC. A sample of his statements on time was: "Do not lessen the time of following desire, for the wasting of time is an abomination to the spirit."

Bible Scholars agree that the Book called **"Ecclesiastes"** of the Old Testament was written by Solomon, the son of King David. **His thoughts in Chapter 3:1-8 on the question of time apply to almost every aspect of life:**

"There is an appointed time for everything, and there is a time for every event under heaven:

There is a time to give birth, and a time to die.

A time to plant, and a time to uproot what is planted.

A time to kill and a time to heal.

A time to tear down, and a time to build up.

A time to weep, and a time to laugh.

A time to mourn, and a time to dance.

A time to throw stones, and a time to gather stones.

A time to embrace, and a time to shun embracing.

A time to search, and a time to give up as lost.

A time to keep, and a time to throw away.

A time to tear apart, and a time to sew together;

A time to be silent, and a time to speak.

A time to love, and a time to hate.

A time for war, and a time for peace."

The Judæo(Jewish)-Christian concept is that **time** had a beginning, created by God. It also assumes that time will end when Christ returns to earth in the Second Coming to judge the living and the dead.

The Christian view is that God's World is Uncreated and Eternal, and His Kingdom exists outside of time and space. St. Augustine, who authored the famous book **"The City of God"**, applied this concept to World History.

A specific amount of time - for example from 11 to 12pm on the very same day - is experienced quite differently by people depending on their circumstances. Time can literally appear to be flying by when someone is excited by something like an interesting movie or at a very enjoyable party. On the other hand, time feels like it is dragging and is very slow to someone waiting in a long line to pay for their groceries.

In general, **time** seems to slide by more quickly as one gets older, since a senior is not as fully aware of what is going on moment by moment like a very active 5 year old. Ask any mother or grandmother who is watching over young children.

CHAPTER 15

FORGIVENESS: THE KEY TO FREEDOM

Forgiveness is unknown in Heaven, where all is *one*, abiding in Everlasting Peace and Love. The need for forgiveness would be unthinkable. Whether we believe it or not, we have never left the Eternal Kingdom and we are really not here; we are *dreaming* that Planet Earth is real. God, however, generously gave each of us a **Free Will**; a dangerous gift and a risk on the part of our Heavenly Father and Creator. Some of the Children of God with their free will, *chose to* **dream** or have the **illusion** that they were somewhere else.

It also means, that while they were still in God's Eternal Kingdom, they could allow a part of their mind to be asleep in Heaven and thinking that they were also here on this planet. What they were doing is called a **split-mind**. If you believe that Planet Earth is Real and you are really here, *forgiveness* is a necessary correction for all the mistakes that you believe you have made. We, as human beings, have to forgive ourselves for believing in the ego and its unreal world.

Forgiveness is the great learning aid in bringing about this thought reversal. However, the Course has its own definition of what *forgiveness* means. We do not just forgive someone who offended us. That is obvious, but not complete! *True forgiveness* means that we have to *forgive ourselves* for any thoughts of separation we have about Planet Earth or any other person living here. On Planet Earth, we tend to forget that all of us are Eternal Siblings of the Heavenly Father. We are

God's Creation: the *One Son* having millions of Siblings.

Forgiveness is also the means by which we can remember who we are and the false thinking of the world is reversed. The forgiven world becomes for us the *Gate of Heaven* by which we remove all feelings of fear, sin and guilt and become *free*. By acknowledging Christ in all our Brothers and Sisters, we recognize His Presence in ourselves.

Let's say that I have a thought about Osama Bin Laden. He must be a hateful person. He caused the death of many people. He still hates America and wants the El Quaeda to punish the United States. That's a terrible thing he did! I can forgive him, because he is one of my Siblings in Christ. I also understand his convictions about America. He grew up in the Middle East. He sees America as a giant that takes advantage of other countries. He believes that the United States will come running to help you if there is *oil, money or something beneficial* to America. He believes that the CIA does all kinds of dirty work abroad.

Actually, I can forgive him by seeing this whole picture from his viewpoint. *But it is much harder to forgive my personal thoughts about him.* If I had such thoughts as prejudice against him and the Arab extremists and if I, an offended American, desired a counter attack, revenge, aggression or war, those vengeful thoughts would have to be forgiven. (*The Truth* is that I am an Arab myself and both of my parents came to America from Lebanon. I love everyone on Planet Earth as my Brother and Sister.)

Do you know that Osama Bin Laden, Hussein, Hitler and every criminal on Planet Earth are our Siblings and God is the Heavenly Father of us all? Can we hate God's other Children who have chosen to become criminals? No, but we certainly do not have to approve of their way of life!

Unfortunately, in the United States alone, there are well over a million of our Siblings in prison. In an effort to keep order in this world, there are Laws of Justice that must be obeyed...and criminals have to pay for their crimes, even in the dream.

It means, in reality, we all share in one Life as God's Children. There is no other life! We came here into this illusion, the ego's world of separation, for several reasons, one of them being here to learn more about ourselves through conflict! Each of us has a distinct Identity that will never be taken away. We are not like a drop of water which has it own identity apart from the ocean, but when that same drop of water becomes part of the ocean again, it actually loses its identity.

You and I are quite different. We were created as an extension of God's Spirit. Even though the Heavenly Father created an unbelievable number of Children in the One Son, we can never really lose our unique Identity. *The Father knows each of us by name!* What God creates is Real, Eternal and can never be threatened. It should come as no surprise to you that, at this very moment, we are still in God's Eternal Kingdom. No one has ever left God's Kingdom. I have echoed this fact several times in this book. *We are there forever.* It is impossible not to share in God's Eternal Realm, called

Heaven. There is no other alternative: GOD IS ALL THERE IS!!!

We came on Planet Earth by using our *Free Will* which allows us to *dream* of leaving God's Kingdom and being somewhere else. In this case, we are dreaming of being on Planet Earth, a world of separation which is unreal and a misuse of God's Divine Power. We should be thankful, however, to our Heavenly Father, Who from beginning, gave each of us a distinct Identity that will never be taken away.

The Truth is that God knows everything and anything that is REAL. Any adjective cannot possibly describe the Infinite and Eternal God. Nothing exists outside of God's Eternal Kingdom!!!

There is nothing else in the world, there is nothing else in the universe or in any other universes, as some believe.

Nothing else exists but God. God is all there is! Why? Because Only God and His One Son (our Siblings, including ourselves) are the only Beings Who are Eternal.

In my fifty years of counseling, some people amazed me when they felt terrible for what they did or said to God. I recall one lady who was very upset. She said, "I struck out at God; I am sure God is very angry with me and will make my life miserable."

I replied, "What can you possibly do to Our Heavenly Father? You think your sins or faults can hurt Him or affect Him in any way? God is invincible and God loves you as His dear child."

Sometimes my mind continues to reflect on the Creator of all that exists. God abides in Eternal Peace and Joy for all Eternity. It is not possible for a mere creature to upset the Almighty and Infinite Creator. We cannot hurt God. God is all there is! There will never be what *God is not...* except when referring to a dream or an illusion which is not real in the Mind of God!

Even thinking for a single moment that we can live a life separate from God, is clearly impossible. If we share in God's Eternal Love, there is nothing to fear.

FEAR AND DIVINE LOVE do not exist in the same person at the same time to the same degree, just as you do not have light and darkness at the same time. The absence of light is darkness. Is darkness real? No! Darkness does not exist. It is only the absence of light!

The absence of Love is Fear, not hate. Fear does not exist. It is only the absence of Divine Unconditional

Love. The kind of love that has no conditions.

If you show fear toward anything in this dream, this illusion, you make it Real, and, unfortunately, the fear becomes more powerful than yourself. But, in reality, nothing in this world is more powerful than you are. You are a million times more powerful than anything on this planet, because you are one of God's Divine Children. Jesus said if you have faith, even the size of a tiny, little mustard seed, you could say to that tree, "Jump in the lake!" and it would. "Move, mountain! And it would!"

We have tremendous power within us. But it is hidden, because we follow the senses of the body rather than the Spiritual Reality within us: namely, the *Mind* and the *Spirit*... which share the Power of God, Our Heavenly Father.

CHAPTER 16

AN ACTUAL AND SURPRISING EYE WITNESS TO THE ONENESS OF GOD'S SON

Once in my whole life, I was able to see us as one. It blew my mind to see the **Reality of Oneness** in that room. This took place in the Cafeteria temporarily used as a Hall of Most Holy Trinity School. One of the speakers was already giving his talk. I had some business to take care of in the Parish House, so I arrived late.

I opened the door to the Cafeteria and what I saw was unbelievable. Everyone became one Spirit. They were all joined as one. I looked and I too was part of the oneness. There were no forms visible. Therefore, I could not see individuals. There were at least a hundred people there, but I could see no separation dividing them into separate identities. It is difficult to explain, but it would have been accurate to say "There was only one of us there."

This was not just a quick flash in time. Rather, I watched for a long time. I did not want to disturb the speaker, so I enjoyed the reality which was present in that room. All were one in God.

The Workbook (Part II,14.1) emphasizes the oneness of God's Son:

> "I am God's Son, complete and healed and whole, shining in the reflection of His Love.
>
> In me is His creation sanctified and guaranteed eternal life.
>
> In me is love perfected, fear impossible and joy established without opposite.

I am the holy home of God
Himself.

I am the Heaven where His Love
resides.

I am His holy Sinlessness
Itself,

for in my purity abides His
own."

God has only *one* Son. Since all of
His Creations are His Sons (before there
were males or females), there is an
infinite number of Children in God's
Sonship.

"We are these Sons of God. As Sons,
we do not each have our own unique Self.
Instead, at the core of each Son is the
exact same Self, a universal Self which
the Course calls the Christ. Christ is
the Self the Sonship shares." All is
one. There is no separation possible!

The fact that we have the five senses of the body and they indicate in every way that we are separate from each other, makes the ego very happy. We can touch one another, see one another and hear one another, all indicating that you are separate from me. This belief is strengthened every day, as our bodies seem to be so real and so separate. Our eyes tell us you are there, I am here! It all adds up to each of us being separate, but that is not true! We are all **One**... Siblings sharing in God's life.

In this world, nothing is as it seems to be. Nothing in this world. If we take this tape recorder, the mantel piece, your hands, the carpet, a book, a glass of water, etc. and break them down into molecules and atoms and sub-atomic particles, they all look alike.

What we would be looking at are simply the building blocks of *form*. They are like tinker toys that are made of wood. All the **forms** that kids are having fun building, would be made of wood, having different shapes and sizes.

All creation is the substance of God, but the *forms* are not Real. The Substance of God is Real, but what you see is a misuse of God's Substance, building forms that can change, that are temporary, can be threatened and, therefore, do not actually exist. The forms are like toys children put together.

Nothing you see with your eyes is real. **Form is not real**, but the Essential Substance from which form is made is Real. And there is only one Divine Substance throughout the universe... God!

CHAPTER 17

SINCE PLANET EARTH IS NOT REAL, WE NEED DIVINE HELP TO GUIDE US HOME

We live in a world which is a misuse and a misunderstanding of God's Power. I have been to many workshops in the past. In the 1950s and 1960s, one of the first questions asked and discussed was why were we on this planet and how did we get here? The story of Adam and Eve *was simply Jewish History*. It obviously was not World History, since Lemuria, Atlantis, Egypt, Babylonia, Sumeria and Greece took place long before Jewish History.

Why did we choose to be born on **Planet Earth**? The Lord Jesus answered that question in 1965. Among other things, we are here to *experience life by* learning to control or discipline ourselves in these unreal and physical conditions of conflict. We are learning to become more and more perfect so that we can awaken and actually enjoy our true Reality as God's Image and Likeness forever.

Jesus said, **"Be perfect as your Heavenly Father is Perfect."** This is achieved with Perfect Unconditional Love. When you experience this Divine Love, you can live joyfully in this life knowing that the Creator has sent a Guardian Angel to watch over you, and the Holy Spirit and the Lord Jesus to guide you. You can live without fear even in the dream! The only thing we need is to have complete Trust in Our Heavenly Father Who knows all things and is Present everywhere.

Jesus states in Chapter one, in His Message, "A Course in Miracles" section 3.1:

"I am the only one who can perform miracles indiscriminately, because I am the **ATONEMENT** (It means that Jesus is in charge of the *correction of errors.*) Jesus continues: **"You have a role in the Atonement which I will dictate to you.** Ask me which miracles you should perform. This spares you needless effort, because **you will be acting under direct communication.** Recognize your errors and choose to abandon them by following my guidance, which can lead you to the highly personal experience of revelation."

"Revelations are inspired by me, because I am close to the Holy Spirit and alert to the revelation-readiness of my Brothers (Siblings). The Holy Spirit mediates from higher to lower communication, keeping the direct channel from God to you open for revelations."

"I stand at the end in case you fail temporarily. My part in the Atonement is the cancelling out of all errors that you could not otherwise correct. As you share in my unwillingness to accept error in yourself and others, you must join the great crusade to correct it. Listen to my voice, learn to undo error and act on it. Miracles correct errors. Miracles occur naturally as expressions of Love. The real miracle is the Love that inspires them. In this sense, everything that comes from Love is a miracle."

"All miracles mean life and God is the Giver of Life. His Voice will direct you very specifically. You will be told all you need to know."

Having heard the Voice for God a number of times, I am not saying that I am better than anyone else. I am vulnerable and I can still make some terrible choices and mistakes in this lifetime. Even St. Paul said "Pray for me lest I become a castaway!"

Some day when you come to that point of listening only to the Holy Spirit and you have learned to live continually with forgiveness in your heart, you will become a Spiritual Master. And you will no longer need to continue doing the same thing over and over. You will be led to your next level under the Guidance of the Holy Spirit and the Master Jesus.

Some people base their entire belief in the Bible only and not on the tradition, background and development of Christianity. **They overlook the fact that Jesus has never left us.** Not for a moment! He is even quoted in the Bible as saying "I will be with you all days (every day) until the end of the world."

I do not expect a Second Coming of Jesus since He has always been present. I know this from personal experience. Also, I do not expect a big show-down between the Lord Jesus and some powerful, evil leader in our future world. *THE LORD JESUS IS THE MOST POWERFUL BEING IN THE UNIVERSE!* He could just wave His hand and the battle against an evil, world-wide leader deceiving many followers, would end immediately.

TWO APOSTLES OF JESUS CAME BACK TO SUPPORT THE MESSAGE OF JESUS TO THE WORLD.

In the book "The Disappearance of the Universe", two Apostles, St. Thomas and St. Thaddeus, appeared to Gary Renard. Gary was sitting at his desk one day and instantly on the couch, across from him, appeared two beings whom he presumed were from the world of spirit. They were in the form of a man and a woman. They were not like ghosts. They were in physical form; he could actually touch them. Gary asked who they were and why did they appear to him. The woman said, "I was St. Thomas, the Apostle, and I wasn't a Saint then, although the church thought I was, because I was an Apostle. The other one was Thaddeus and he came as a man. They said that they had many life times. In the illusion, they reincarnated in Gary's future and in that future time, both of them became Ascended Masters during the same life-time when they were together. They both reincarnated often together.

Having become Ascended Masters, they no longer had to come back again and were now able to enter any period of Human History. There is no possible evil that can harm them. Why? Because they stepped out of the dream, the illusion that we mistakenly call Reality.

In this state, there is no fear, no anger, no guilt, no war, no violence, no sickness and no death. Gary Renard's book is designed to lead you, regardless of where you are spiritually, to understand "A Course in Miracles" and explains it in a language that is easier for the average person to comprehend. The three books of ACIM are a little complicated unless you are already involved in Metaphysics. Ask anyone who has studied it. The verses are written in iambic pentameter, a literary and poetic form. It is very challenging.

It does not repeat what was dictated for clarification and there is no need to correct itself. To live the Message of Jesus is our goal in life. We are truly Saints if we achieve that goal. We made it! We have fulfilled the purpose of life here. I have asked my Guides if Mother Teresa and Fr. Solanus Casey lived their lives according to the teachings of Jesus. I got a positive response for both of them. They both were very holy and were operating on a higher dimension. They were superior beings!

Every civilization has had Great Masters. At the time of Buddha, Moses, Rama Krishna, Jesus, Hermes Trismagistis or St. Teresa of Avila, the Holy Spirit has always supplied the average person with examples given by the devout and dedicated ones.

Unfortunately, most enlightened human beings are often misunderstood and even attacked by their enemies! So, it comes down to this as Jesus pointed out in His Message: you have to choose between the ego and the Holy Spirit, that is, choosing between what is real and what is unreal. If your heart and soul are filled with the Divine Love of God, you are ready to let go of the illusion and remember your intimate relationship with our Heavenly Father and Creator! You will have arrived! That is your ticket out of this mess.

This is a very savage world conducted by the ego. If it were God's world, do you think that we would have to struggle to stay alive, that our bodies would grow old and die, criminals would appear to succeed, that we would be eating other things like animals and plants to survive or people would be killing other people? Impossible!

This cannot be God's world or God's creation. That would make God very vicious and cruel. It would be an insult to Almighty God Who creates only what is Eternal! Everything you see here on Planet Earth is temporary and easily threatened. The only thing eternal on this planet is our Spirit, which has never left God's Eternal Kingdom.

We will always be One with our Infinite Creator, but having a *Free Will*, we can *dream* of being on Planet Earth. It is only a trick and an illusion of the mind! Remember the Message of Jesus: ***"We are on a journey without distance to a place we have never left."*** We have never left God and we cannot! There is nothing else that is Real but God. And God created us in His Image and Likeness.

It was an insane idea and we made it more difficult for the Holy Spirit to transform our minds and guide us back Home.

Open your eyes and enjoy the Truth. We belong to God's Family and we always will. There is no death, there is no time...God is all! And where God is, we shall always be!

You now have an idea how blessed and how powerful we are as God's Divine Children. God loves us just as any parents would toward their children; however, in this case, we were created Eternally Perfect by the Divine Creator of all Life. And His Love never ends.

If I were a parent, I would always love my children. If they make mistakes, I don't care. I would still love them. If one of them ends up in jail, I would still love that kid. If another ends up on drugs, I am still going to love my child and help in any way I can. In the same way, if we make mistakes, God still loves us. He doesn't give up on us. And God is a Perfect Parent! A Perfect Parent would never give up on His children. We were created in God's Image and Likeness as

His innumerable Divine and Eternal Children.

And some day when you can so align yourself to God's Spirit, the Voice for God and live daily the teachings of Jesus, you have no idea how much joy is going to fill your heart and your soul when you leave this illusion.

Nothing has ever happened in this life that can be compared to the mystical and spiritual joy that your Soul is going to experience. But if you do not keep moving in that direction, you are going to keep believing the same thing over and over in the dream that is filled with changes and distractions until you make a decision to rise above this level to a non-dualistic world where all is one in God and you are a part of God's Eternal and Delightful Kingdom of Heaven forever.

Oneness is simply the idea that "God is". And in His Being He encompasses all things. When we say "God is" we cease to speak, for in that knowledge the use of words become meaningless.

Beyond the body, beyond the sun and stars, past everything you see and yet somehow are familiar with, is an arc of golden light that stretches as you look into a great and shining circle. The light expands and covers everything, extending to infinity forever shining and with no break or limit anywhere.

Within it, everything is joined in Perfect Continuity. Nor is it possible to imagine that anything could be outside, for there is nowhere that this Light is not.

This is the Vision of the Son of God, whom you know well. Here is the sight of Him who knows His Father. Here is the memory of what you are.

God is the First Cause and Creator of all Life. God is Perfect Love and Unity and not a body, neither male nor female. The Holy Spirit yearns to share its Being as the Creator did. Creating by sharing is the will to create. It does not wish to contain God, but wills to extend His Being.

It should be noted again that God has only one Son, His Divine Creation. As one Son (an infinite number of Children), each of us is an integral part of the whole Sonship. There was never a time when all that God created was not there. GOD'S THOUGHTS, BEING ETERNAL AND UNLIMITED, WILL BE THE SAME BEFORE *TIME* BEGAN AND AFTER *TIME* IS GONE. Being one of God's Eternal Children, we are beyond all harm, separation or imperfection and held forever within His Holy Will.

Heaven is not a place nor a condition. It is merely an awareness of Perfect Oneness and the Knowledge that there is nothing else outside this Oneness.

In Heaven is everything God values, and nothing else. Everything is clear and bright and calls forth one response. There is no darkness and there is no contrast. There is no variation and there is no interruption. There is a sense of *PEACE* so deep that not even a wild imagination or fantasy in this world can come close to what it is like in Heaven.

The Oneness of God and his One Son is a reflection of this important principle of ACIM, *"Ideas leave not their source"*. Christ is God's Son as He created us, uniting us with one another and with God as well. We are the Thought which still abides within the

Mind that is our Source. As the One Son, we have not left our Eternal Home nor lost the innocence in which we were created. We abide unchanged forever in the Mind of God and we always shall.

God knows everything! What God does not know cannot exist. The Almighty and Infinite God creates only what is Real and Eternal, for thoughts endure as long as does the Mind that thought of them. And in the Mind of God there is no ending nor a time in which His thoughts were absent or could suffer change. God's Mind is forever one, Eternally united and at peace.

This world is the opposite of Heaven and everything here takes a direction exactly the opposite of what is True. In Heaven, the meaning of Love is known. Here on Planet Earth, the illusion of love is accepted in Loves's place and is perceived as separation and exclusion.

The ego is simply an idea that harm or change could happen to the Son of God without His will.

CHAPTER 18

EVOLUTION OR
INTELLIGENT DESIGN?

In the August, 2007 issue of the U.S. Catholic magazine, there was an article written by Francisco J. Ayala, called *Monkey Business*. Ayala is a professor of evolutionary biology and philosophy at the University of California-Irvine. He is an expert in the field of Evolution and he speaks strongly in defense of it.

The title of this chapter is an effort once again to discover the origin of the human race. Did we evolve into our human form or was there an intelligent designer of the human body, since our bodies could not have happened by chance.

Evolution is the history of living things, including the origin and the development of life. With the recent discovery of DNA, we can now trace our history all the way back to a common ancestor. It is based on *natural selection*, which explains why we have eyes for seeing, hands for grasping and legs for walking. These are facts in today's world, just as we now know that the earth has an orbit around the sun. Centuries ago, it was believed that the whole universe revolved around Planet Earth. That is far from the truth! Only an ignorant or twisted mind would believe that today.

Being a Catholic priest, I wanted to know what the Catholic Church had to say about evolution. In 1950, Pope Pius XII in his encyclical stated that the Teaching Authority of the Church does not forbid research and discussion concerning evolution as long as the human body comes from pre-existent and living matter - "for the Catholic Faith obliges us to hold that souls are immediately created by God." (That was once believed over fifty years ago).

In 1996, however, Pope John Paul II said in his speech to the Pontifical Academy of Sciences that there is no conflict between evolution and the doctrine of faith. Evolution has been well proven, with evidence coming from many different disciplines. Those who are working on the study and interpretation of the Bible need to be well informed on the latest scientific research. Of course, he also adds that the human soul or anything spiritual could not have come about by evolution. There has to be some other way to explain the soul.

(He apparently had not heard of Jesus' message in 1965 about the origin of human soul and the *One Son* of God).

Pope Benedict XVI in 2007, stated that evolution implies questions that must be assigned to philosophy and reaches beyond the realms of science. That is very true and is the essence of Jesus' message.

This brings to mind that all of creation is the Substance of God, but the forms are not. The forms are not real. The Substance of God is Real, but what you see is a misuse of God's Substance. Anything made of forms like the human body, a train or a car can change. They are temporary, can be threatened and therefore do not actually exist. The forms are like toys with which children put together and build things. Nothing you see with your eyes are real. Forms (or outward appearances) is not real. Divine

Substance is Real. And there is only one Eternal Substance in the universe... **God.** We live in a world which is a misuse and a misunderstanding of God's Power. Not being real, that is why we do not know why we are here. I have been to many workshops in the past. One of the first questions asked and discussed in the 1950s and 1960s was, "Why are we here? Why are we on this planet and how did we get here?"

I have learned since that we are here to *experience!* We are learning to experience *joy, anger, violence, pride, revenge, despair and learning to control or discipline ourselves in these unreal conditions.* We are learning to become more and more perfect so that we can some day be awakened by the Holy Spirit and the Lord Jesus. Then we can actually enjoy our true Reality as God's Image and Likeness forever.

Jesus even said, "Be Perfect as your heavenly Father is Perfect." This is achieved with Perfect Unconditional Love. When you experience True Unconditional Love, there is no fear in you. This is one sure way of recognizing Perfect Love. It's not easy to live without any fear, fear of being mugged, fear of pain, fear of being hit by a car or falling and break your hip, or spraining your ankle, acquiring a disease or an illness, getting a heart attack, losing a lot of money and so on. Fear is the absence of love. That's what it's all about.

Beyond this, learning cannot go. When we are ready, God Himself will take the final step in our return to Him. The split-mind will no longer exist and we will be as we always were: the *One Son* in the Eternal Kingdom.

Once you make the right choice and live it, you are on your way Home. And when all of us have chosen the Holy Spirit and the Lord Jesus as our Divine Guides and there is no longer a need to hide in this unreal world or illusion made by our Siblings' Collective ego, then we will no longer need this planet or the millions of planets, galaxies and star systems that make up whole, physical universe. The illusion of the universe will quietly disappear. At that point, we will all be in our true Eternal Home, and...yes, I won't have to write any more books about going Home! And this is so!

To order additional copies of **"PLANET EARTH: As Human Beings, Where Did We Come From? Why Are We Here?"** or any of the other books by Father Jay Samonie, please complete the following page and mail form with check payable to:

Rev. Jay Samonie
34666 Spring Valley Drive
Westland MI   48185-9457

Name (Please Print)			

Address			

City, State, Zip			

Telephone (Include Area Code)			

Qty	Title	Price	Extend
	On My Way Home	14.95	
	Reflections on My Way Home	14.95	
	My Greatest Joys on My Way Home	14.95	
	The Holy Spirit: Our Divine Companion Guiding Us on Our Way Home	14.95	
	The Rite of Passage	14.95	
	PLANET EARTH: As Human Beings, Where Did We Come From? Why Are We Here?	14.95	
Sub-Total			
Mich Residents Add 6% Sales Tax 90¢ Per Book			
Shipping & Handling ($3 Per Book)			
Total Enclosed (US Dollars Only)			